Stock Market

Investing

Blueprint

Your Best Stock Investing Guide. Simple Strategies To Build A Significant Income. Perfect For Beginners(Forex, Dividend, Options Trading Information)

Blake Holt

information contained within this document, including, but not limited to, — errors, omissions, or inaccuracies.

TABLE OF CONTENTS

information contained within this document, including, but not limited to, — errors, omissions, or inaccuracies.

TABLE OF CONTENTS

information contained within this document, including, but not limited to, — errors, omissions, or inaccuracies.

TABLE OF CONTENTS

DESCRIPTION

Professional investors and traders have taken the time to learn and utilize the right information. They know where to go to get the information they need to make the critical decisions they have to make to put their hard-earned money to work in the live markets.

All successful traders I know have put the market in perspective and only do what they know to be true. They are willing to take what the market is going to let them take out of it on a daily basis. This is a very important characteristic to develop. It also goes back to not being too greedy when in the live market.

To be successful in this business it is recommended that the proper education and training be done. All professional investors and traders I know have done it and so should you if you would like to attain a level of consistency that the professionals all have. With all the information in this guide, I am certain that you are destined for greatness in the stock market. Here are some of the things you will learn here:

- How to buy and sell stocks
- Investing in stocks and bonds
- How to create a timeline for systematic investing
- Picking the right stocks
- Various trading strategies you should employ for success
- Position trading tactics

- Value investing
- Investment risks
- Mistakes to avoid and
- Tips for success

Grab this copy today and learn more on how to invest and succeed in the stock market. What are you waiting for?

INTRODUCTION

Most beginners' investors and traders have quite confused ideas when approaching the stock market, investing in stocks (or options, ETFs), commodities etc.) or trading in general.

One of the pivotal points that creates confusion in the mind of those interested in making their money work through investments is the lack of understanding of the crucial difference that exists between trading and investing.

The confusion derives from the fact that in the eyes of the investor or the uneducated and non-conscious trader, doing trading or investing seems to be the same thing.

In reality, although they are united by the desire to make a profit, the two operations arise from different logics and follow different rules.

In fact, those who invest in a measure of the value of what they buy (an action, a house, a business, an object of art, etc.), try to buy it at a discounted or otherwise balanced price, and the entire operation is based on the prediction or hope that, over time, the good purchased will increase in value and that this increase in value will automatically be reflected in a corresponding increase in its market price allowing it to be sold for a profit.

An easily understandable example of investment is that of those who buy agricultural land in the expectation that it will then be buildable. The greatest investors of history, such as the legendary Warren Buffett, are in fact masters in buying depreciated quality. Of course, their time horizon is never very short and the value of what they have purchased can remain or even go down for a certain period of time without this causing them to worry excessively.

Who trades, however, does not bet on a change in the value of things. To be honest, the hard and pure trader does not care highly about the objective quality or the nature of what he buys, he is only interested in acquiring it at a price that (in a generally rather short time frame) he plans to grow, regardless of the fact that the value of what he purchased remains perfectly identical.

BUYING, SELLING AND OWNING STOCKS

When it comes time to prepare to make your fist trade, you are going to need to consider the way you are going to purchase stocks that is right for you and to finalize a trading plan that you can commit to in the long-term. Only by ensuring these things are in order will you be able to get started with the odds in your favor.

Buying stocks

The primary way that most investors go about purchasing stocks is through a brokerage. Brokerages broker deals between buyers and seller while also charging a fee for each trade that is made on top of taking a commission from the results as well. There are two types of brokerages that you will see most frequently, those who offer a variety of services such as trading advice and those that offer a more barebones approach, which are typically online only. Full service brokerages typically have a historical record of successful trading and by using one you will be responsible for less than if you go with an online approach. They are always going to cost you more than online brokerages, however.

It can be difficult to compare various brokerages to one another, simply because it is easy for them to spin their various strengths and weakness in different ways.

Nevertheless, you are going to need to persevere as finding the best brokerage for you can easily mean the difference between the success and failure of your stock market investment plans. Specifically, you are going to want to take note of specific fees structures as well as the services that the brokerages offer in order to ensure that you are in the best position to take advantage of what is available to you. Additionally, you are going to want to want to compare margin rates, commissions, word of mouth, account minimums and any promotions they are currently running.

Instead of going through a brokerage, you may be interested in investing in stocks through a dividend reinvestment plan (DRIP) or direct investment plan (DIP). These plans allow shareholders to purchase stock for a given company, from that company directly. To get started with these types of plans you need to purchase shares of a given stock that pays dividends and then reinvest those dividends back into the company in exchange for additional shares.

Preparing a plan

In order to put together a successful trading plan, the first thing you are going to need to consider is what sector of the stock market you want to focus on first. Sticking with one broad category of stocks, at first, is going to make it much easier for you to do your required research. When it comes to choosing the right sector of the market, you are also going to consider how much you have to start investing with, the length of time you are looking to go before making a profit and the type of return on your investment you are hoping for.

With these specifics in mind, you are going to then be able to determine how much risk you are comfortable with taking on in order to see the types of results you are looking for. If you don't like what you come up with, you can either change the amount you hope to generate as profit, the amount of risk you are comfortable with or the amount you have to invest right off the bat. The overall result is always going to be a result of these three factors.

In order to ensure the trades that you make don't head south you are always going to want to go ahead and set stop losses for all of your trades, no matter how much of a sure thing you have reason to believe it might be. A stop loss is a preselected point at which you will sell off your shares if the price moves too low or too high in order to prevent additional losses. The closer a stop loss is to the amount you entered a given trade at, the less you will lose on a high-risk investment.

Furthermore, you are going to need to consider the point where you are going to be willing to walk away from a given trade because you have made enough of a profit from it. Rather than striving to squeeze every cent possible from a given trade, it is important to consider an exit point that finds a balance between profitability and risk. If you find a stock that is proving to be so profitable that you don't want to exit at the predetermined mark, then you can instead sell off half of your holdings at that point and set another exit at a point of greater profit to split the difference between risk and reward.

In order to determine if your plan is successful, the first thing you are going to need to do is give it some time to generate real results. Based on the time frame for profit you determined previously, you are going to want to wait and gather enough data to ensure that you are likely to turn a profit using your plan in the long-term. During this time, you are going to want to take detailed notes including when trades were made, what factors went into your consideration for the trades, the costs and if the trade ended in success. Keep in mind that anything above 50 percent will eventually turn a profit given a lengthy enough timeframe.

Most importantly, if you find a trading plan that works for you, you are going to want to stick with it as diligently as possible, even if your emotions are telling you to go a different way. When trading, your goal should always be to minimize the effect that emotions have on your actions as completely as you can. Trading successfully is all about the numbers which means that emotions are only going to get in the way and almost always end up doing you more harm than good. The more robotically you can execute the trades you are looking for, the greater your profits are going to be across the board. If you find yourself considering making a trade based on emotion, take a moment to ask yourself if you would make the trade if your emotions weren't a factor and then make a choice depending on the answer.

Researching stocks

In order to invest in a stock with confidence, it is important that you research just what exactly you are getting yourself into. This means you are going to want to consider several company documents, outlined below.

10-K: The 10-K form is a form that every publicly traded company needs to file yearly and it outlines everything major the company experienced in the previous 12 months. This should be the first thing you look at as it will give you an overview of the company in question. You will also want to check the 10-Q forms which break down the 10-K into quarterly increments.

Proxy statement: The proxy statement is a public statement that gives you information of the shareholder proposals, board of directors, and management compensation breakdown of a given company.

Annual report: The annual report is a yearly document that includes statements by the higherups in a company to give you a high-level view of where the company has been for the past year and where the top brass thinks it's going.

Financial statements: For every company you research you are going to want to look up their balance sheet, income statement and cash flow statement as together these three will give you a good financial overview of the company.

Historical Data: While the most recent information on the company is going to be useful, you are also going to want to look into the historical data on the company to determine if where they are at currently is a fluke or if it is the result of years of hard work. This means you will want to take a look at the above documents for the last five years.

Purchasing stock

Once you have done your research, and found a few stocks that fit your plan, you will want to go ahead and actually place your first trade. The execution of a trade can be more complicated than you might expect which is why the following with break down these concepts. First things first, you will want to keep in mind that executing a trade refers to a specific transaction while using the term trade in other contexts can refer to the type of trading plan or strategy you are using.

Based on the current state of the stock in question along with the research you have done, you are either going to want to go long on (buy) or go short on (sell) the stock of the company you have been research. When you place a trade through your brokerage platform, that trade then goes out via their trading network and connects you with another person who is willing to complete the transaction based on the specifications you set. The brokerage you are working with may also have shares of the stock in question available if you are looking to buy. You will then need to pay any relevant fees, plus a commission to the brokerage for the privilege of using their service. It doesn't matter what type of trade you are making; you will also be dealing with the following types of orders.

Market order: This is a request that you send that sets off the transaction that will result in buying or selling. You don't have much control of this request as the market is going to dictate the price you can expect in the transaction.

Limit order: If, based on your research, you like the look of the direction the stock in question is moving you can set a limit order which says you will buy or sell when the price reaches a certain level specifically. This helps to negate the issue of volatility.

Stop order: This is the request to sell off all of your shares of a specific stock if the price hits a precise target. This should be set for every trade at a point just above where holding onto the stock becomes unfavorable.

Stop limit order: This is a combination of the above, and it keeps all aspects of a given stock's movement under close watch for specific triggers.

Trailing stop order: This is more versatile than a standard stop and will only trigger if the price falls to a specific amount of a preset total as opposed to when it reaches a given price. If you are looking to make truly long-term investments then these will be your best choice as you can set them based on your overall level of risk assessment.

STOCKS AND BONDS

Most beginners are either confused or scared when they hear about investing in the stock market. This happens majorly due to the lack of an understanding of how stocks and bonds work. Your misconceptions and pre-assumptions need to go away if you want to become a consistent investor and build wealth. As you have decided to enter the world of the share market, you need to be familiar with the two most important financial instrument, which are: stocks and bonds.

There is a vast difference between stocks and bonds, which most beginners are not able to understand.

So, this chapter will focus on giving you a foundational guide on stocks and bonds.

Stock provides ownership, while the bond is a debt.

For companies, organizations or any other entities, bonds and stocks are two ways of getting funds for their business and operations.

When you buy a stock, you get a piece of that company. The entity offers you a part of the company and asks for cash in return.

On the other hand, you get a bond by lending some money for a particular period of time as a debt. The entity promises you additional interest on the money you lend.

Stocks are also known as the shares of a company. Shares are the portions of a company sold to get funds for different reasons, such as expanding the business, completing a vast project and so on. Buyers of stocks or shares become partial owners of the company the stocks belong to.

On the other hand, bonds are simply money you give to a large corporation, government body or other entity as a debt. The entity decides to get a loan from the investors in the public market and promise a particular interest on the money. The bonds come with a maturity period, which is the time when the investor receives the complete amount back. Before that maturity period, bond owners keep being paid the promised interest. In rare cases, bonds default, which makes issuers unable to give back the money.

For an owner of a stock, a company's loss or profit becomes his/her loss or profit. This means that you have to share the risks with the company as a stock investor, but this risk pays off in the long-term.

Unlike stocks, bonds can't give you long-term returns. However, they enable you to get a steady income. With stock investments, the risks are lower. The market prices can fluctuate, but the bonds give you back the whole principle along with the interest. In some rare cases, some bonds default.

Stocks

When you hold stocks of a company, you become part owner of that company. You can also purchase shares of a company stock and obtain benefits whenever the company stock prices increase or the company provides dividends. In the case of liquidation, shareholders get a chance to claim the assets. However, the shareholders can't own those assets.

Stockholders obtain the right to vote during shareholders' meets and get to have dividends whenever declared. However, if the stockholders own a preferred stock, they can only obtain dividend preference but not any voting rights. Also, the owners of preferred stocks get to claim more assets in case of liquidation.

When a company performs well and grows, the stocks of that company go up, and this increases stockholders' invested wealth. Self-service platforms as well as broker services offering stock buying services for investors also exist.

Beginners have many questions when it comes to stock investments. The main ones are the following:

Which stocks are perfect to buy right now?

Can you tell me about a particular company in terms of investment?

How can I know if a stock price is right or wrong for me?

As a beginner, you need to relax and go slow with your stock investment. Start by understanding how to evaluate a stock and choose one for investment.

How To Choose A Perfect Stock

You can begin by creating a list of companies that you use on a daily basis. For example, your list can look like this:

- Technology: Microsoft, Apple, Snap
- Services: UPS, IBM
- Transportation: Ford, Tesla, CSX
- Entertainment: Netflix, Disney, Live Nation

Similarly, you can make a list of more companies. This way, you can look beyond the clutter of over 5000 stocks and think only about the most-valued companies. However, a good company does not necessarily mean a beneficial stock.

To evaluate and select a stock, you have to go beyond your favorite brands and companies. This evaluation should involve:

1. Trend analysis

Looking at the growth in sales is a reliable analytical approach to understanding the trend of a company. You can look at the sales from the last year, last 2 years, last 5 years, and more. Comparing the sales history helps to know if there is a steady growth in the company trend in the market. If the graph seems to go up and down, it creates confusion regarding the performance of that company. Reducing trends are definitely a red signal, so you need to choose a company with increasing sales.

2. Scope of products

This requires great levels of involvement in the market. You need to stay updated on product development and future demand for the same type of product in the market. Stay up to date with market news to find out if a product or service will be growing in demand in the coming future. You should select the stock of a company whose products or services seem bright in the near future.

3. Per-share revenue, growth, earning and profit

These are the financial pillars of any stock. Understanding these can seem difficult initially, but there are various online platforms that offer visualized evaluations of stocks with respect to revenue, growth, earnings, and profits. Practicing regularly will make you get the hang of it.

4. Signs of insider trading

A major indicator of insider trading is if senior executives of a company are investing major amounts in company stocks. Company executives have faith in the future of that company, which means you can trust the stock. Similarly, if a company's top executives are selling most of their company stock, you need to become aware of it and sell the stocks too.

5. Management capacity

When you are selecting a stock to invest in, the internal work culture of a company matters too. A capable management with a good philosophy ensures profitable turnover. The company should also be able to execute their philosophy and showcase positive management capabilities.

Thanks to the internet, you can obtain all the information required for free. So, it comes down to your determination in doing as much research as possible. If you doubt any of the given factors, you need to stay away from that stock.

Looking at balance sheets, earnings, and various charts will confuse you. However, you will eventually start making sense of them and stock evaluation will definitely become easier.

If you follow this process and choose the perfect stock, you can make a lot of money. However, this only happens when you choose a stock from a market you understand. A product type, sector or demographic, which you are knowledgeable on will help you find the best-performing stock for you.

Despite all these great features, there is still a disadvantage. The performance of the stock depends on the performance of the company, so if you pick the wrong stocks to invest in, you can get poor returns. Stock investment is not diversified, which makes it crucial to pick solid companies to get stable returns.

Bonds

Bonds are a type of loan you offer to an agency or company, where the receiver promises to give periodic fixed interest along with the return obtained according to the face amount of that bond at maturity. The federal government, corporations, municipalities, states, and government agencies usually issue bonds too.

Generally, a bond issued by a corporation can have about $1000 face value. The corporations usually choose a semi-annual period to pay the interest amount. The interest you attain via bonds come within the taxes, however, you can save tax by investing in the municipal bonds, as the interests obtained for them do not come within the federal taxes. In some cases, these bonds are also free from state taxes if you are a resident of the state that issues the bond.

Just like buying stocks, you can buy bonds via companies as well as via a secondary market, and their value depends on various factors including the direction of the interest rate. The price of a bond increases with the decrease in the interest rate direction. In other words, the bond prices are inversely related to the prices of the interest rates.

When you try to look at it initially, you may feel that this phenomenon is quite illogical to behave in such a way. However, when you look closer, it does make sense. For you to understand it easily, you can try to understand the concept of zero-coupon bonds. These bonds do not pay in coupons, but deduce their value obtained from the difference between the par value (the face value of a bond provided at maturity) and the cost price.

Here is an example to explain this concept:

If you find a zero-coupon bond being traded at $900, with a par value at $1000 (which is paid to the bond bearer after a year of maturity), the interest rate on the bond presently is at 11.11%, which is calculated by: (1000 − 900) ÷ 900 then multiplied by 100.

A person, who has to pay a sum of $900 for such a bond, must feel satisfied at the received rate of interest of 11.11%. However, this satisfaction is not limited to just this calculation. It is further dependent on the fluctuations in the bond market.

On average, you can obtain about 1.5% interest rate from a bond that has a duration of 2 years.

As an investor, bonds give you unique benefits:

- You get way more stability in bond investments than stocks.
- Your returns are guaranteed, which keeps you stress-free regarding the money you invested.

The stability factor also makes bonds low in their return capacity, which means that bonds offer smaller returns compared to the potential returns of investing in stocks.

So, who should think about investing in bonds?

If you are the type of investor (whether retail or corporate) who likes to know exactly how much return you will get, bonds are the right choice for you. Anyone, from young to old, can invest in bonds. The stability of these investments makes them reliable. The returns are usually low, but they are fixed and unaffected from the volatility of the stock market.

Apart from knowing the exact amount of return, you can also choose a suitable time period of investment, and you can invest bonds for 1, 2, 5 or more years. If you stay invested for longer periods, the return rates increase.

Buying bonds and selling them may seem a little more difficult than stock trading, especially if you are trying to invest in bonds individually. In addition, once you find a bond to invest in, your money becomes blocked for the chosen period of time. If you want to take your money back before the agreed time, you need to pay a penalty.

So, you can choose stocks or you can choose bonds, and it all comes down to how much research you do before making the choice. A key rule that works for everyone is low-cost and diversified investment. For instance, if you are 22 years old and start investing $500 per month, this is a low-cost investment. With this investment, you can do your research and choose a diversified index. That way, you will become a millionaire by the time you get to your 60s.

For many investors, both stocks, as well as bonds, are important, and finding the right balance of bonds and stocks is the right way to create a diversified investment portfolio. You can decide the percentage of stocks in your portfolio according to how much you can tolerate risk.

How Do Bonds Affect The Stock Market?

Bonds have the power to influence stock markets, but both bonds and stocks act as contenders for the invested capital. While a bond is the safer option between the two, its return is lower. Thus, when the value of stocks goes up, the value of bonds goes down.

For the booming economy of a country, the value of stocks will rise. Customers from that region buy substantially, leading to higher earnings for the companies because of the rise in demand. Investors' confidence levels rise due to the upsurge in the market. They desire to tackle inflation by buying stocks and selling their bonds.

Furthermore, when a country's economy is slow, customers purchase at a lower rate. This results in low profits for companies, with a decrease in the rate of stock prices. This obligates investors to choose bonds for investments, as they can still expect a low but regular interest from the payment.

Oftentimes, bonds and stocks rise together in the market as well. This can happen because of various reasons, which you will learn in upcoming sections of this chapter. Also, stocks and bonds can fall together. That indicates chaos in the market, and it forces investors to sell all their and stocks and shares. However, in such times of panic, gold prices rise. So, with negative effects, you will find positivity in other areas. All you need to do is observe the market and identify the investment opportunities that will make a profit.

Understanding Stocks and Bonds

In simple terms, bonds are loans that you give to a private or public organization, and the interest you get from it stays fixed throughout its tenure period. In the end, the company gives you the principal amount, if it does not default. The S&P ratings of the firm can inform you of whether there is a chance this firm defaults.

Nevertheless, as time goes by, the value of a bond keeps changing, but this will only matter to you if you are planning to sell your bonds in the market. Traders who deal in bonds compare the returns of bonds with other bonds. This process is known as yield. Therefore, bonds that have low S&P ratings, and poor rates of interest are worth lower than bonds with higher yields.

Stocks, on the other hand, are shares of a company that you own. Their value depends on company earnings, which are issued every quarter. In addition, the value of stocks keeps fluctuating every day. This value is dependent on future trading estimates in comparison to the values of other companies in competition.

Bonds Vs Stocks: Which One Would You Prefer?

Choosing whether to invest in a stock or a bond is based on two aspects.

One: What personal objectives are you planning to accomplish? If you do not want to consider your invested principal amount as expendable, do not want to bother with inflation rates and expect regular returns, then bonds are the way to go. Bonds could be the right choice for you if you are reaching the age of retirement or are just accumulating an income for investment purposes.

If you are still holding your stocks at the time of recession, do not require an income and just want to beat the inflation, then stocks should be your preferred investment choice. Furthermore, stocks are great for investors who are young and have high-paying jobs as they can invest a portion of their income in stocks.

Two: How is the economy running? This also means that you need to know the state of the economy in your region. If the economy is booming, then stocks could be lucrative, as stocks start increasing in value as consumers purchase more goods. If the economy is going down, then bonds are the preferred option for you, as bonds will safeguard your investment money while offering you a fixed but regular interest.

The majority of financial planners suggest that diversifying your portfolio is a lucrative investment strategy. This means that you should invest in a mixture of bonds and stocks to limit your risks and maximize gains. Also, studies predict that diversifying your investment portfolio will ensure maximum returns without increasing the risk of losing money.

The role of Federal Reserve To Boost Stock Market

In the U.S., the Federal Reserve is responsible for regulating interest rates via market operations. When it wants interest rates to go down, it buys the U.S. Treasury. This method is similar to raising demand for bonds in a country, which causes their price to go up. Eventually, when the value of bonds increases, interest rates decrease.

A decrease in the interest rates forces the stock prices to rise. This happens for two reasons.

One: Individuals who buy bonds will now be able to get a lower rate of interest (with a low purchase return as well). This may trigger them to purchase stocks with higher earnings, but with higher risks as well.

Two: When the interest rates are low, it is cheaper to borrow money. Companies who are looking for investors can expand their departments to produce more goods and services. Furthermore, it also helps people purchase new assets, including houses, cars, education, furniture, and other amenities at a lower price. Ultimately, low interest rates help boost the economy, as it increases corporate profits as well as stock prices.

When Do Bond and Stock Prices Fluctuate In Opposite Ways?

Generally, bonds and stocks travel in the same direction. However, this may not always be the case; when this correlation starts to behave abnormally, investors start to panic, because it is a sign that there will be a major change in the market, and it may cause heavy fluctuations.

So, why does this happen?

• **When there is a rise in stocks, but fall in bonds**

Stock values rise when there are signs of growth or improvement in the economy. This happens due to a rise in profits, which causes the stocks to rise in value. However, this can also lead to inflation. Due to a rise in stocks, the prices of bonds tend to fall. This compels the Federal Reserve to raise interest rates in order to regulate them. Increasing rates causes borrowed money rates to increase for companies. Therefore, the bonds they issue to investors have to be provided with a high rate of interest. As a result, the bond market collapses as these bonds pressurize the existing bonds to yield, causing heavy changes in the rates of old and new bonds. Nevertheless, the profits may still increase with a rise in stock values and fall in bond values.

• **When there is a rise in bonds, but a fall in stocks**

Even though there are plenty of reasons for a fall in stocks, the most prominent one is the slow decline of an economy, and even the belief that an economy is slowing down can trigger this. This triggers investors to purchase more bonds than stocks, causing the rise of bond prices. Investors do this as they want to stay on the safe side. This increase in bonds causes a decrease in interest rates.

Another event leading to a decline in stock prices and a rise in bonds is when the Federal Reserve decreases interest rates, which usually happens when there is a recession or chances of a recession. This leads to an increase in the current price of bonds, which causes the bond price yields to fall in order to match the new bonds. This technique is used by the Federal Reserve to stir investments, which leads to high-earning stocks and increased profits.

Why is this important to investors?

It is important to keep a lookout for fluctuations of bond and stock prices away from each other to keep track of changes in the market. For instance, a rise in the price of bonds can cause panic among investors, as it indicates that the market is about to face sudden and rough fluctuations.

When do bonds and stocks rise up in the same direction?

We have just seen when and why stocks and bonds sometimes move in the opposite direction. Now, let's have a look at when they both rise in the same direction.

When the stock market is deteriorating, investors start to see the risks involved in investing in stocks. Therefore, to stay on the safe side, they withdraw the invested capital and place it in bonds instead. This eventually causes a rise in the price of bonds. Once stocks recover and risks are lower, investors choose to switch their investments back to stocks, which leads to an increase in their price. Sometimes, such an oscillating scenario can cause both bonds and stocks to rise together.

Here are a few situations where there may be a mutual rise in both stocks and bonds:

• **Dubious perception about stocks**

Sometimes, the stock market functions quite efficiently, but still keeps investors doubtful, as they feel that rising stocks may fall in price at any moment. In this situation, investors continue to invest in stocks while also investing, resulting in the rise of both their prices. Investors invest in a way to avoid losses if the stock prices fall, which results in high prices for both stocks and bonds.

• **Relying on corporations and the government**

Investors think that federal organizations and firms which supply bonds will have the ability to pay the interest rates on bonds even at the times of a fall or recession. This perception increases the value of bonds. Meanwhile, companies that issue stock also seem to grow due to the confidence built upon them by investors. Therefore, when investors rely on both stock and bond-issuing companies and agencies, their values tend to rise together.

• Low Interest Rate

When interest rates stay low for a long period of time, bonds remain the same in value, while an increase in interest rates results in a decrease in the value of bonds. This happens because, with the increase in interest rates than the prices at which a bond is supposed to compensate, investors are able to acquire better returns with the newly issued bonds as interest rates are high. This means that they will skip the existing bonds and choose new bonds due to high returns. Similarly, when the interest rates are low, bonds tend to stabilize or increase in value, as investors are not able to find better rates with new bonds. Meanwhile, stocks are also appealing to investors as the interest rates are stable. This can cause bonds and stocks to rise together in price.

• Decrease in inflation rates

Increasing inflation causes a downfall in prices of both stocks and bonds. With a rise in inflation rates, firms have to spend more on supplies, products, and raw materials, and this decreases their profit margins. Ultimately, this makes investing in bonds and stocks dangerous. However, when there is low inflation, the interest rates from bonds can compensate investors to ensure profits. This results in investors being attracted to bonds as they increase in value. At the same time, as companies retain profits due to low inflation, their stocks are also attractive to investors. Companies that profit from such a scenario tends to grow their stock prices, and this causes both bond and stock prices to rise.

CREATE A TIMELINE FOR SYSTEMATIC INVESTING

In this chapter, we are going to be taking a close look at how you can plan your investment strategy in such a way that you can determine your goals and what you need to do to achieve them.

Consequently, the importance of creating a timeline for systematic investing boils down to managing your expectations so that you can set a realistic time frame for your goals.

Thus, the first step in this process is determining what your goals are.

This might seem like a no-brainer. However, you would be surprised to see how many folks get into investing without having a clear goal in mind.

Often, you hear folks say that they want to "make money" or "get rich". But, what does that even mean? What does it mean that you "want to get rich"?

The fact of the matter is that having a clear goal in mind is the first step toward achieving success in investing and trading. If you know what you want to accomplish, then you can begin from a realistic starting point. You know what you can do and what you can achieve.

Based on that, a realistic goal might be as simple as "not lose money". I know that's pretty vague, but it was my goal when I first started investing. I made up my mind that while I felt comfortable with investing, I would be determined not to lose any money. I am happy to say that I was successful at that from the get-go.

Therefore, start out with small steps. Goals such as:

- Supplement my income

- Make some extra money

- Learn how to make money from day trading

- Become so good at day trading that I will be able to leave my job one day

And so on will help you to focus your mind during your learning period.

Why shouldn't you set a monetary goal?

You shouldn't set a monetary goal because you don't know how much you can make until you actually begin trading. You can't set a target of "$1,000" a month since there are many variables which you won't be able to control from the outset of your trading endeavors. It won't be until you actually begin trading that you can gain a good sense of how much money you can realistically. Based on that, you can set monetary targets and work toward reaching them.

Determine How Much You Can Invest

Once you have a clear goal in mind, the next step to take into consideration is knowing how much you have to start off with.

If you are going the day trading route, this starting amount might well be determined by the minimum requirements that brokerage accounts demand of investors.

For instance, you might sign on for an account which will have a minimum deposit of $1,000. Thus, you need to fund your account with at least $1,000 before you can begin investing. Other accounts may ask you to deposit more. Nevertheless, there are accounts which have minimum funding of $500.

Now, bear in mind that you need to look at this money as if you were going to Las Vegas; you need to be prepared to lose it all at the craps table. The reason for this mentality is due to the need of becoming emotionally detached. Thus, if you have an emotional attachment to your initial investment, you will engage in emotional trading rather than trading based on logic and fundamentals.

As such, the more money you are able to start off with, the more your initial profits may be. However, you also need to take care and not succumb to the temptation of going all-in at the beginning of your trading endeavors. If you do, you certainly run the risk of losing everything before you even have the chance to make some profits.

Understand the Various Types of Investment Approaches

Investing in the stock market isn't just about opening an account and buying stocks. It takes a certain understanding of the various ways in which you can allocate your investable assets.

For instance, you might choose to become a passive investor. In this case, you can purchase mutual funds or contribute to your 401k. This is a long-term approach, but it is a great way to make your nest egg grow. While the returns may not be spectacular, over a 20 or 30-year period, you can see your investments take shape.

For more aggressive and involved investors, day trading can become a feasible option. Day trading will allow you a lot more control over your investments in addition to making some potentially impressive returns. Whatever your ultimate investment approach, it is important that you understand the ins and outs. That way, you can make the best-informed decision based on your goals and your specific needs.

Set a Target Date

This might be just as hard to set as a monetary amount. However, it helps to have a finish line in mind. For instance, you might think to yourself that you would like to save up enough money for a new car within 6 months. Of course, if you plan to buy a Lamborghini, then you might have to set some pretty lofty goals. But if your goal is to purchase a new

Chevy, then you might not have such a steep hill to climb. It's all about understanding what your goals imply and how you can get there.

If your goal is to save up money for a down payment on a house, then you can figure out how much money you are going to need and a realistic timetable. For example, you might feel that saving $25,000 in one year is doable. So, off you go to invest until you reach your goal.

Setting a timetable is a psychological trick that will help you focus. If your plan is just to save up for a down payment on a house but with no timetable, then you won't have a sense of urgency. Having a timetable creates a discipline that will help you keep your eyes on the prize.

Ask for Help

One of the most common pitfalls when setting up your investment timetable is not asking for help when you need it. While it is perfectly normal to get stuck at some point, begin able to recognize when you need help is essential in order to ensure that you are able to move forward.

Being able to count with other folks who have been through the same experience as you is certainly useful. In addition, knowing a good accountant which you can trust is also a great idea. A good accountant can help you assess taxes and other bookkeeping issues.

So, be sure to surround yourself with other folks you can rely on in case you ever need a point in the right direction.

DAY TRADING

In this chapter, we will focus on day trading and how you can get started day trading stocks and various other financial assets. In addition, we will discuss some pitfalls which you need to watch out for when day trading.

As we have defined earlier, day trading refers to trading stocks and other financial assets with the singular characteristic that these assets are bought and sold within the same trading day. This is an important distinction to make as other trading approaches advocate holding on to positions for longer than a single trading day.

Within any trading approach, you will find two types of positions: open and closed. In essence, when you hold a stock, you have an open position. When you have sold off a stock, you have closed your position. Bear in mind that day trading is all about holding positions open for less than a trading day. In some cases, open positions may refer to a few hours or even a few minutes. Regardless of how long you hold an open position, the point is to hold it long enough to make a profit.

Often, day traders are content with holding a position long enough to make a small profit per share. This profit may be as small as a few pennies per share. However, you can multiply your profits due to the volume of shares you have traded.

Consider this example:

You have bought 1,000 shares of ABC company at $5 a share. You are expecting the price to go up by the end of the trading day. As it turns out, the price of the shares goes up to $5.50 per share. Naturally, you are inclined to sell at this point. Now, you might think that 50 cents per share is not much, but when you multiply it over 1,000 shares, you have a profit of $500. That's not bad for a day's work.

In this hypothetical example, what you have earned is a small profit per share but becomes a considerable gain when multiplied by the larger volume of shares. This is what makes stock trading a profitable endeavor.

The biggest pitfall to consider at this point is the temptation of hitting a home run. I am sure you have heard stories of folks who buy up stock at a low price and then have it skyrocket. These investors clean up and suddenly become wealthy overnight.

While that is a dream for many folks out there, the fact of the matter is that hitting a grand slam is improbable. What is a tried and true formula is buying up stocks and selling them for a profit as many times as possible? Consequently, high-frequency trading is one tactic which can help you multiply your earnings, however small, over a longer period of time.

How to Get Started in Day Trading

If you have made up your mind to become a day trader by this point, then I would like to welcome you to a world filled with a great deal of excitement, but also filled with a great deal of uncertainty and volatility. Nevertheless, you can thrive in a structured system.

Day trading's main advantage lies in cutting out the middleman, that is, cutting the need for a stockbroker. Stockbrokers generally charge high commissions for something which you can learn to do with just as much as skills as they have. The main difference lies in that you have your best interest in mind while most stockbrokers have their company's best interest in mind. Hence, cutting out the middleman, in this case, stockbrokers becomes one of the best decisions you can make.

However, you still need to rely on a duly licensed brokerage institution. Bear in mind that this is due to the fact that the general public cannot trade stocks on a stock exchange. Consequently, there is a need for a brokerage institution to facilitate their capabilities to individual traders.

Thus, the first step is to open a brokerage account. This is what will enable you to begin trading stocks and other financial assets. When you open a brokerage account, you will be granted access to that institution's trading platform. What that means is that you will have the opportunity to use their trading software to make your deals.

Now, there are two types of brokerage accounts:

1.   **Full-service account**. This is the account that comes with all the bells and whistles. They are characterized by having unlimited access to all trading functions, access to all types of financial assets and high-level data and analytics software. Most of the time, these types of accounts will allow you to have real-time access to stock quotes and other relevant data. They come with a higher maintenance fee in addition to commissions per trade. Since you are paying a higher maintenance fee, it is quite probable that you will have to pay a lower trade fee.

2 **Discount brokerage account**. This type of account does not come with all the bells and whistles. In fact, it may be limited to the basics of the trading platform and not much else. In addition, your access to data and analytics may be restricted. You might get information with a certain delay, say information refreshed every five minutes or every ten minutes. Now, you *might* think that that is not a big deal, but in the world of day trading, especially if you are working with razor-thin margins, a five-minute delay on stock quotes may represent the difference between making a profit and missing out on opportunities.

In addition, you will have to consider the fees that are associated with opening up a brokerage account. So, I would encourage you to read the fine print in the contract you sign as there might be a small fee, that over time, will add up. Naturally, the more fees rack up, the lesser your profit will.

Here are the most common fees that you will have to pay.

• **Maintenance fees**. When you sign on to your new brokerage account, you will find that you have to pay a maintenance fee. This fee is associated with the cast of keeping the show running. It generally covers the cost of the platform itself in addition to the data and analytics that come with your account. Most importantly, it is often a one-time fee, such as annually. Therefore, you need to see how much your chosen brokerage institution will charge you for maintenance as most full-service accounts do have a higher fee associated with them as compared to discount brokerage accounts.

• **Membership fees.** Some brokerage accounts, though not all, may charge you some akin to a membership fee. What this entails is, most commonly, a one-time charge in which you are just paying to play. This fee would be separate to your maintenance fees though it could just be bundled into your maintenance fees. A sign-up fee might be charged initially with discount brokerage accounts. If you do have to pay this charge, then it pays to see if it is a one-time payment, or if it is an annual fee. Bear in mind that most full-service accounts will have some type of membership fee attached to them.

• **Commissions.** While you are not hiring a stockbroker to conduct trades for you (as a day trader you would be doing this yourself), you would not be required to pay a broker commissions for the returns they produce on your portfolio. However, the brokerage institution may still charge you a commission over the returns you get in a given time period.

While this is not common with day trading account, it would be a good idea to double check anyway. That way, you can be sure that you won't be surprised with any commissions charges billed into your account statement.

• **Trading fees.** In addition to maintenance, you will have to pay fees per trade. For each trade, you will have to pay a flat fee as opposed to a percentage-based fee. Most trading accounts advertise a low fee that ranges from anywhere to $2 to $6 or even $7. The general rule of thumb with trading fees is that full-service accounts will have a lower trading fee given the fact that you are already paying a maintenance fee. Discount brokerage accounts will generally have a higher trading fee as you are either not paying a maintenance fee or a very small one. Therefore, they need to recoup their overhead by charging you a higher fee per trade. If you are planning on becoming a high-frequency trader, that is conducting a high number of trades per day, then you might want to look into an account that gives you a trade bundle (such as 25 trades for $25). This can help you get a grip on your transaction fees.

• **Taxes.** While this isn't something that the brokerage institution would charge you (you are liable for sorting out your own tax bill), you will more than likely be on the hook for paying your fair share of taxes. So, I would encourage you to check with a trusted accounted to see what kinds of taxes you would be on the hook for. Most likely, you would be on the hook for income tax. Nevertheless, stock sales are subject to capital gains tax in most states. So, as part of your due diligence, check to make sure you pay any, and all, taxes you are liable for. The job news though is that some states offer tax incentives as being a day trader may fall under the category of "investor". So, you would get some additional break that normal folks would not be entitled to.

Getting Started with Conducting Trades

Once you have your account sorted out, you would be ready to start trading.

However, I would like to make a very important point in this regard: do not start trading with real money from day 1. The reason for this is that if you are new to trading, then you will most likely have a few bad deals at the beginning. Sure, it is possible to have beginner's luck, but the fact of the matter is that you will most likely lose a few trades before finding your bearings and really making the most of your opportunities.

This is why I always advise folks to try out a demo or practice account before fully committing to their chosen trading platform. By testing out the platform through a demo account, you can trade with monopoly money, but on the real system. This will enable you to find out which aspects of the account really work for you. In addition, you'll be able to see which aspects of the platform don't really work for you. In the end, you will be able to make a decision based on what you feel is right for you.

In addition, trying out a demo account lets you see if the claims brokerage institutions make are real. For instance, you will hear advertising about how user-friendly their platform is or the "intuitive feel" of the system. You will have a chance to test drive it before putting any money down.

Beyond the test drive, it gives you a chance to begin seeing how trades work and how you can lose money. Yes, that's right. The practice account gives you the opportunity to get hammered while you play with monopoly money. That way, when you make your way to the real deal, you are ready. Personally, I will take the opportunity to learn through losing any time I don't have to pony up real cash. Naturally, it is a lot harder, and a lot more painful, when you lose your hard-earned cash.

Most trading platforms offer free demo accounts for a period of around 30 days. After that, you either have to fund your account with real money to keep playing, or you will have to officially sign on. Make sure that you are aware of how much your chosen brokerage institution will require you to pay down. Most accounts will have a minimum requirement of $1,000 though you might hear some discount brokers advertise buy-ins of around $500. So, that could be a good opportunity for you to get started with little money down.

Additionally, you will find that most discount brokers will offer you a bundle of free trades when you sign up. These are the trades you need to take advantage of since you can make some good money without having to pay the transaction fee. Now, imagine if you wasted free trades on bad deals. Do you see the importance of having a good demo account?

The only pitfall, in this case, would be to do the demo account on one platform and then switch over to another for the real thing. The issue with this approach is that you might find yourself with two different systems. If that we to be the case, then you might find yourself losing out on some deals while you get used to the new platform.

If you should happen to try out a platform and decide it's not for you, you can always switch something else. In that case, I would advise you to take the free demo account with the new platform you are looking to switch to. That way, you can take the time to get acquainted with the system without actually losing any money in the process.

What to Look for in a Trading Platform

Thus far, we have talked about trading platforms.

Please keep in mind that the brokerage account is one thing while the trading platform is a completely different one. The brokerage account is just your official ticket into the game. The trading platform is where you will actually make the magic happen. Consequently, it is the trading platform that should feel as comfortable as possible for you.

So, here are some things to look out for when you are testing out a new trading platform.

- **User-friendly.** Make sure that the platform feels comfortable and easy to use. Most platforms will allow you to toggle your views. That way, you avoid having a cluttered screen. Rather, you can display the information you want to look at when you need it. If you find that it is too complicated for you to use, then you might want to have a look at another platform just to compare.

• **Integration with other platforms**. Make sure you find out if the platform you have chosen is integrated with other platforms. If so, this can basically afford you the opportunity to have unlimited options in terms of stocks and other traders. If it doesn't then you might find yourself with a very limited pool of stocks and traders.

• **Data and analytics.** Also, check out to see what type of data and analytics the platform has to offer. Ideally, they would offer your real-time data which you can use to compare. If it doesn't, then you might want to consider purchasing a premium membership to information which does offer real-time data. Otherwise, using data that is on a delay will cause you to make decisions based on flawed information as it would not reflect the market conditions at the time you are making the trade. This is important to watch out for. So, make sure to double check to see what data and analytics your chosen account offers.

• **Automation.** Virtually all trading is software-based now. So, make sure you find out what automation features your trading account platform offers. The basics include being able to set up automatic buying and selling. Also, see if it can repeat the same transaction several times over and if it can conduct multiple trades at once. While you might not be conducting high-frequency trading or making multiple deals at once right away, after a while, you will find that automation is a nice feature to have.

Initially, you will find that just getting a handle on the software is a challenge. Nevertheless, your experience with the platform itself will boost your productivity and your results. This is why you need to take the time to become familiar with the platform itself. That way, you can feel confident and secure that you are making the right deals.

Do take the time to go through all of the tutorials. Some platforms may offer you coaching sessions included in the price of the account. So, take advantage of those opportunities during your demo period. As such, you can go through the rigors of learning how to use the account while you are still playing with monopoly money and not when you are playing with real dough.

TRADING STRATEGIES TO TRY

Starter Strategies

Breakout **Strategy:** This is a common strategy employed by traders new and old. The main idea behind this strategy is that you chose a price point for a given stock that, once hit, will indicate enough of a positive swing to justify buying more of the stock. When using this method, it is important to consider a price point as well as the amount of time you are willing to give the stock in order for it to reach that price point. This is a strong strategy to employ if the market is moving in a certain direction and ensures you will always know when to jump on the bandwagon.

This strategy is an effective choice if the market is currently or was recently at either a drastic high or low. To complete this strategy properly all you need to do is set an order that is either above the high or slightly above the low and then play the averages. If the market is not moving strongly in one direction or another, then this strategy can easily backfire as prices are more likely to stick to prescribed ranges. If there are not strong signs of trending use with caution.

Retracement strategy: To properly implement this strategy, it is important that you are able to determine a likely pattern for the price of the stock to continue trending towards. To take advantage of this fact you wait for each price increase before the inevitable decrease which comes as some people sell and others try and trade the opposite. You sell on the high and use the profits to buy back in at an increase of shares under the assumption that it will rise again. Then you simply repeat until you are no longer sure of the increase.

This strategy will only work effectively when there is something major enough to cause ripples across the market that are not felt all at once. This strategy will become less effective the more unsure you are about additional jumps in price and should therefore always be used carefully. You may be tempted after seeing a single large jump from a stock to try and employee this strategy but beware of using it flippantly. Stay strong and you will turn a profit.

Buy and hold: The buy and hold strategy is a type of passive investment in which, as the name implies, shareholders buy into a stock that has strong long-term potential and then hold onto it even when the markets see a downturn. This strategy looks to the efficient market hypothesis for success which states that it is impossible to see above average returns when adjusting for risk which means it is never a good idea to resort to active trading. It also says that seeing decreases in value in the short term is fine as long as the long-term trend remains positive.

This strategy is very effective when it comes to minimizing the commissions and fees that you have to pay a brokerage because you will only have to do so once before generating an eventual profit. In this strategy, you also don't have to worry about timing the market which is useful for new investors as determining when to buy low and sell high can be much more difficult than it first appears. In practice, the effectiveness of this strategy can vary wildly, depending on when it is acted upon.

Stock split strategy: Pay attention to companies that declare a stock split. What is a stock split? The best way to understand how it works is with an illustration: If you have 100 stocks of company X at $30 per share and a stock split is declared, you will end up with 200 stocks at $15 per share. As you can see, the number of shares increases while the price per share decreases corresponding to the split. Also, a stock can also be split into three or four, etc. So, how is this a good strategy?

Most companies that declare a stock split are those that are doing well. The value of their stocks gets so high that they need to split it in order to welcome more people to invest. Investors usually do not like stocks that already have a high price, so a stock split is made. The key here is to identify and examine the companies that declare a stock split. It the split is legitimately made, then chances are that the price of the stocks after the split will soon increase due to the good performance of the company.

You should also be aware of the reverse split. Take note that a reverse split is a bad thing, so you should stay away from it. Here is an example of a reverse split: Let us say that you have 50 shares at $10 per share. If a reverse split is made, then you will end up with 25 shares at $20 per share. As you can see, there is a decrease in the number of shares and a corresponding increase in the price per share.

Companies that use a reverse split are those that are struggling to survive in the market. This is why you need to be careful when you notice a reverse split. Also, you can see that the price of stocks increases, which makes it look like as if there is growth or development in the company. However, the truth is that the increase in the price of the stocks is only caused by the company's own manipulation of the price and not because of any legitimate growth. Of course, there is still a chance that the company may do well after a reverse split, but the risk is just too high. It would be better if you invest your money in something else.

Price action trading: While many active traders make use of complicated indicators that have to do with reading charts and drawing figures based on complex formulas, as a new trader you are likely going to be much better served by starting with price action trading instead. While some new traders may turn their noses up at anything that professional traders aren't currently using, the reality is that indicator based trading only works for the experts because they have already learned how to compensate for its flaws. As such, if you are brand new to the process then you are going to want to start with something that can be understood easily and work on improving your trade percentage before you need to start worrying about finding more complicated ways to pick the stocks that you ultimately do trade.

At its most basic, price action can be thought of as a way for a trader to determine the current state of the market based on the way that prices are currently acting as opposed to what one of the dozens of different indicators has to say about it after the fact. As such, if you are a trader that is interested in getting started as quickly as possible then sticking with price action trading, for now, can save you serous time as you only have to spend your time and focus studying the market as it is in the present. Additionally, focusing exclusively on the price and the price alone will help you to avoid much of the unnecessary information that is constantly circling the market, blocking out the static and increasing your overall chance of success.

To get started using price action to determine when to trade, all you are going to need is the basics that come with the brokerage and trading platform you have chosen, starting with price bars. A price bar is simply a representation of relevant price information for a set period of time, typically in units of 5 minutes, 30 minutes, 1 hour, daily or weekly. In order to create an accurate price bar, you need four different pieces of information, the first the is the amount the stock in question opened at, the second is the overall high for the day, the third is the overall low for the day and the fourth is the price it closed at. This data is then plotted in such a way that each day forms a box with a line through it.

What this type of strategy provides you with is a clear idea of what the levels of resistance and support are like for the time period in question. This, in turn, allows you to pick trades with a higher degree of certainty. All you need to do is keep in mind that if demand is stronger than supply then the price is going to increase, and vice versa. If the movement indicates that this is likely to continue in the same direction then you will want to pick the point where it is likely to happen again and use that as your entry point. If the opposite is true then you are going to want to sell ASAP to prevent yourself from losing out on gains you have already seen. If the price reaches the support level then demand will exceed supply and if it reaches the resistance level then supply will exceed demand.

Turtle trading

Turtle trading is not about a "slowly but surely attitude". It is more about riding the big trends in the markets. You see, everyone wants to hit a home run. Everyone dreams of coming up to the plate with the bases loaded and just knocking the cover off the ball. Sure, it is a great fantasy. One big deal and you are set for life.

However, get-rich-quick almost always burst in your face. In the best of cases, you will end up putting a dent in your portfolio. In the worst of cases, you could be wiped out. As such, turtle trading does not espouse a risky trading approach in which you are betting on making a huge splash.

Consequently, turtle trading is not the sexiest of approaches. It is not a run and gun approach that is the hallmark of maverick investors and stockbrokers. In fact, it is rather boring as turtle trading espouses having a solid understanding of the fundamentals that support the trends and movements in prices, be they up or down.

Core beliefs: Given that turtle trading is more philosophy and mindset than a quantitative model, there are a series of core beliefs that are espoused by this approach.

They are listed as follows:

1. Keep your emotions in check even when your capital is bouncing up and down

2. Keep A Cool Head

3. Judge yourself by your processes and not by the results themselves

4. Be prepared to act when the market strikes

5. Be ready for the impossible at any time

6. Plan ahead for the next day; be aware of what your plans are and your contingencies

7. Determine the probabilities of winning and losing; determine what you will gain and what you will lose

As you can see, this is a very rational approach. The intent is to remove the psychological and emotional factor out of the equation. Keep in mind that this is about keeping your emotions in check amid the volatility and uncertainty that accompany markets. In addition, "keeping a cool head" is one of the most important traits that all investors must possess. In a way, it is like having ice water in your veins.

Do the math: The first bit of information you need is to calculate the investment's volatility. The inventors of the program used the letter N to represent this number. You may also see the abbreviation ATR for "Average True Range." This is an equivalent term.

They calculated this by figuring out the 20-day exponential moving average of the potential investment's "True Range."

You should plan on using a spreadsheet program to calculate and record the numbers you find while finding the information you need.

To get a day's True Range value calculate:

- Maximum (H-L, H-PDC, PDC-L)
- H = Current High
- L = Current Low
- PDC = Previous Day's Close
- You will also need:
- PDN = Previous Day's N
- TR = Current Day's True Range

Once you have those numbers, calculate them as follows: (19xPDN+TR)/20=N

Since you can't calculate N without already having an N for the day before, create a simple 20-day average for the True Range and plug that in for your first PDN.

Once you have that information, it is time to calculate the Dollar Volatility Adjustment.

This is a simpler calculation:

Dollar Volatility = N x Dollars per Point

Turtle Traders use the term "Units" to describe the size of an investment. The number of units for an investment is calculated as follows:

Unit = 1% of Account/N x Dollars per Point

The point in Dollars per Point refers to the contract size expressed in dollars. So if you were considering a contract for 40,000 bushels of wheat, it would equate to 20,000 points.

The 1% figure is not chiseled in stone. You can tweak it depending on how aggressive you are or how you are feeling about your portfolio.

Let's say you have a portfolio of $500,000 to work with and N= .0141. The formula would work as follows:

Unit = $5,000/.0141 x 20,000

This results in a figure of 17.73. You would buy 17 contracts.

The purpose of all this is to help keep the risk from an investment's volatility within reason. Rather than going with your gut, you have a formula that will help you determine an effective amount. It will also help regulate the size of your positions in trades.

It's also important to work with a large enough portfolio. Too modest an amount will lessen the effectiveness of this volatility management. Ideally, you will want to start with this program with a minimum of $500,000 in your portfolio.

Margin trading

Margin trading is a technique where you borrow money from a broker in the hopes that you will see bigger returns on your money in the form of profit. Essentially, this can be considered to be a situation where you're taking out a loan from your broker. In this way, you as a trader are able to purchase more stock than you would be able to do so otherwise.

One of the first things that you need if you decide to purchase stocks via the route of a margin is to open a margin account. Of course, as a beginner, you should know how a regular brokerage account operates, but you may be less familiar with the ins and outs of a margin account. Margin accounts differ from cash accounts in many ways. One of the first ways in which a margin account is unique is that a broker actually needs your penned signature in order to open one for you.

Secondly, you must have at least two-thousand dollars to invest in a margins account, and some brokerage firms even require that you put more than two-thousand dollars into this account. This minimum two-thousand deposit that you make into this margin account is known as the minimum margin. After you deposit this money, you then have the option of borrowing up to half of this amount. For example, if you opened a margin account and put $5,000 into it, your broker would allow you to borrow up to $2,500 of that money.

Additionally, the $2,500 that is your personal money and is not going to be borrowed is known as the initial margin. It's important to note here as well that some brokerage firms will require that you pay more than fifty-percent of the initial margin. For example, if this were the case in our $5,000 situation, it would mean that you might only be eligible to borrow $1,000 from your broker instead of $2,500. Instead of fifty percent, they would only be letting you borrow forty percent from them.

However, this strategy can backfire when the price of the asset does not go up, and the investor gets a "margin call", that is, they have to pay up. If the investor does not have the money to pay up, then they may be deemed as insolvent. This may lead the investor to be kicked out. In the case of large financial institutions, insolvency is a huge deal and may lead to the bankruptcy of entire financial institutions. So, the moral of the story is to always have enough cash, or highly-liquid assets such as bonds, which can be liquidated fairly quickly in the case of a margin call.

All of this is not to say that trading on margin isn't the right choice for some traders, it is just to make you aware of the risks that are inherent in taking this particular plunge. As long as you never invest more than you can realistically afford to lose, your margin-based risks are mitigated substantially. These risks can be mitigated to an even greater degree by keeping the following strategies in mind.

Long common stock on margin strategy: Buying common stock on margin is a type of leveraged paly with the goal of doubling up on your return on investment for each dollar you put into the stock in question. It is important to keep in mind that your potential for loss is going to be doubled as well, however, so you are still never going to want to invest more than you can potentially afford to lose. You are also going to want to factor in the potential amount that you will have to pay back should the margin trade turn against you and add that to your risk amount as well. If the stock turns against you, it is always good to have a firm line drawn where you will get out before your losses reach a point that you can't realistically handle.

This strategy can be used successfully across all timeframes, but the longer you stay in the greater your anticipated risk is going to be. As such, it tends to be used most successfully in shorter timeframes, both to decrease the potential for risk and to minimize the amount of interest that you are going to have to pay your broker for the privilege of hanging on to their money.

In order to ensure you activate this strategy at the right time, here are a few scenarios where it might make sense to get in while the getting is good:

- When the stock is in the midst of a confirmed uptrend. Trying to pick a stock when it is at the bottom of a downtrend is risky, even if it is near the support level. When margin is in play, going with a relatively sure thing is always the right choice

- When fundamental analysis shows that the company's financial health is viable and indicates that it is likely to remain so in the near future

- If the technical indicators you favor show that the stock is bullish.

- Institutional traders are committing to the stock in question by purchasing it in large quantities

- You have reason to believe that the next announcement the company makes is going to be extremely positive and is only a few weeks away

The sector or industry that the company is a part of shows strong signs that it is currently poised for growth in the coming phase of the economic cycle.

PICKING AN INVESTING STRATEGY THAT SUITS YOU

At this point, you should be clear as to how fundamental investing works, how technical trading operates, and how to pick growth stocks. You also should have a fairly clear idea of how to pick an income stock. Now, with all that knowledge out of the way, we need to focus on a fundamental question.

You already know that you want to do something with that pile of dollars you worked so hard for. Currently, it's in the bank, and you and I know, that that is the worst place for your money. In fact, it's only a step away from stuffing your money into mattresses. The end result is actually the same because banks pay so little interest that inflation, sooner or later, would eat up the purchasing power of your saved dollars.

You need to do something with that money. You should, at this point, be clear as to what your objectives are. Are you trying to protect the value of your money because you're about to retire? Are you trying to grow your money because you're a fairly young person and would like to multiply your cash? Maybe you'd like a nice mix of both? Perhaps you'd like to generate an income from your money? You should have a fairly clear answer at this point.

In this chapter, I'm going to walk you through key selection factors regarding strategies. You have to be as clear about these as possible. They have to make sense as far as your personal set of circumstances is concerned.

You shouldn't invest in stocks a certain way or adopt some sort of strategy just because people you respect and admire do the same. Their particular set of circumstances might be different from yours. Their needs and preferences might be different from yours. You have to adopt a strategy that makes sense to you personally. It has to suit you because this is your money we're talking about.

Assuming You'll Be Picking Your Own Stocks

At this point, we're going to assume that you're going to be picking your own stocks and you're not going to put your money in mutual funds so a professional fund investor will take care of your money for you.

We're assuming that you're not using a professional investment vehicle outside of a mutual fund because, again, in that situation, somebody else is going to be doing the hard calls for you. Instead, we're going to be assuming that you, yourself, will be the only person that would select the stocks that you are going to buy to either protect the value of your money, grow your money, or generate an income, and anything in between.

Assuming that you're going to take ownership of this project, you have to answer the following questions.

How Much Time Do You Have?

How much time do you really have for investing? Keep in mind that investing doesn't just mean picking a stock, buying, and selling. There's a lot that has to happen for you to do that well. You have to buy analysts' reports, you have to read these reports, you have to get all sorts of data, you have to research. You need all this information so you can make a truly informed decision.

In many cases, a lot of these materials are not free. Sure, there are lots of blogs, websites, social media pages that give you all sorts of analysis, but if you really want the good stuff, you would have to pay for it because chances are, the stuff that's publicly available on Bloomberg, CNBC, and similar sites is stuff that other investors have beat to death. In other words, there's really not much movement there if you're looking for solid value.

For example, if you're looking for a growth stock that is a gem that other stock market players haven't fully recognized, it probably would be a good idea to spend a tremendous amount of your own personal time finding such a stock. Otherwise, get comfortable with ponying up a decent chunk of dollars for professional analysts to isolate these companies for you.

What Percentage of Your Investment Portfolio Can You Stand to Lose?

I don't mean to throw water on your plans to grow your money, but we're talking about stocks here. Stocks can go up- and they can also go down. Now with all that said, even if a stock crashes, it doesn't necessarily mean that you lost money.

This is what we call a paper loss. It's only a loss in terms of the actual market value of that stock if you were to decide to sell it today. But assuming that you're not going to be selling, it's just a loss on paper. Things may well turn around and you may have a paper profit on your hands in no time.

With that said, there are certain situations where you feel that you have to liquidate your position. You just have to exit the stock. If that's the case, what percentage of your investment portfolio can you stand to lose? Can you waste $25,000 or 25%? Can you stand to lose a million dollars or 10% of your portfolio?

It really depends on your income, what your other assets are, as well as your overall net worth, as well as the 'emotional value' of your funds. There is no right or wrong answer here. This is truly personal to you.

Some people who are worth billions may turn out to actually have a very low loss appetite. In other words, they can't stand to lose even a hundred thousand dollars. On the other hand, a person who may be worth a million dollars, might actually be okay with losing $500,000 if it means he or she can stand to gain another $2 million.

Again, loss appetite varies from person to person. It depends on how you were raised. It depends on your values and priorities. It also depends on your personality. It depends on your past experiences. It all boils down to risk appetite. And when it comes to this factor, there are really 3 kinds of investors.

Aggressive investors

These are proactive investors who are ready to lose 50% or more of their portfolio value in exchange for the hope that they could gain so much more. We're talking about doubling their money or tripling their money. They're okay with losing half or even all of their money.

Moderate Investors

These individuals believe in putting a cap to the amount of losses that they could potentially suffer from the stock market. This, again, varies from person to person. But usually, a moderate investor tries to cap his or her losses at 33% or lower.

Conservative investors

These are people who either cannot stand too much risk or they're close to retirement. In the latter case, they know that their income will come from fixed sources and they won't be making as much money as before, so they basically have to live on a fairly predictable rate of return.

Conservative investors really cannot mess around with the stock market all that much. As I mentioned earlier, at best, only 20% of your total investment portfolio should be in stocks and those stocks must almost all be blue chips or tried and proven stocks that appear that they won't be going anywhere any time soon.

How Patient are You?

This is a very important question that a lot of other investment books do not ask. I need you to give me a straight answer because you have to be clear as to how patient you really are. A lot of people try to invest in the stock market in a very conservative way. They only invest maybe 20% of their investment portfolio and they try to play really safe stocks.

So far, so good, right? Well, the problem is, they're also very impatient. They have the mindset of people investing in growth stocks while at the same time investing almost purely in conservative stocks. Do you see the disconnect? What's wrong with this picture? So you have to factor in how patient you are.

If you are the type of person who can patiently watch grass grow, chances are, a conservative investing strategy would work out well for you. Even if a stock trades sideways for a long period of time and goes quarter after quarter of almost no visible breakouts, then you'll be okay.

On the other hand, if you're not a very patient person, then you either have to invest in mutual funds so somebody else would do the waiting for you, or you might want to switch your investing strategy to something that fits your temperament.

How Old are You?

Your age, believe or not, plays a very big factor in how you should invest. If you're below 40, knock yourself out with growth stocks. You can afford an aggressive investment strategy if you're in this age range

If you are 40-50 years old, you should start looking at more moderate investment strategies because it's only a matter of time until retirement is around the corner. If you're over 50, you really have no choice but to play things conservatively.

While it's theoretically possible that your nest egg, when invested properly in the right growth stocks can double, triple or even quadruple, it's also just as likely that a huge chunk of your saved assets would go up in smoke. You don't want out in the worst way possible because you're only a hop, skip and a jump away from retirement.

Available Strategies

To recap, what are the stock trading strategies available to you? Again, your selection here depends on the questions I posed earlier.

Fundamental Investing

Fundamental investing is a very powerful and conservative approach to growing your money. The downside is that it requires a lot of time and resources and it turns on accurate data about the company. If you're going by hype, if you're going by reputation, then all bets are off.

Technical Trading

Technical trading requires software. You also need a fast trading platform. You can't be a slowpoke when doing technical trading because the window of opportunity that you're trying to lock into may have passed or disappeared the moment your trade is fulfilled.

You need a very fast trading platform. A lot of big time traders who do technical trading use lightning fast or almost instantaneous trading platforms.

Also, you need to invest quite a bit of your personal attention in technical trading. You basically have to watch the stock you're trading like a hawk so you can see opportunities, jump on them, lock in, and either register a loss or cash out at a profit and then look for the next opportunity.

Technical trading, believe it or not, requires a tremendous amount of discipline because it's easy to think that just because you traded well, that your luck will continue. This is what kills the profits of too many technical traders. They just let their position ride for too long. You should set clear return goals for yourself.

If your goal for the day is to secure a 5% return, the moment you achieve it, stop. Start again the next day. Similarly, if you are a longer-term trader and your goal is to register 10% over a week or more, if you're able to hit that point, stop.

A lot of technical traders often end up reversing or undermining their initial gains because they just can't stop trading.

POSITION TRADING TACTICS AND STRATEGIES

In this chapter, we will look at how you can implement some wise position trading strategies in order to help you reduce your level of risk and boost your understanding of how you can make the most of your investment decisions.

One word of caution: if you choose to engage in position trading, I will encourage you to do your homework on the investment vehicle you are purchasing. In addition, it pays to be on top of every development with regard to your open positions.

Don't be afraid to pull the trigger on a deal if you don't feel comfortable with the way your position is trending. As such, you may have to liquidate your position sooner than you anticipated if you don't feel confident about the likelihood of your security rebounding.

That being said, let's discuss some of the ways you can engage in position trading.

Commodities

Commodities are a good place to start with position trading.

Often, commodities will have sharp fluctuations in the short term but may be poised for long-term gains.

Let's consider oil as an example.

Oil is a highly volatile commodity which depends on a host of factors in order to determine its price. The factors that come into play when setting oil prices boil down to supply and demand. As long as the supply is up, the price will be down. And as long as supply is down, the price will go up.

Oil is dependent on supply as demand will virtually remain the same. If anything, demand will go up when oil is cheaper, and it will level off as it gets more expensive.

Now, when you invest in oil, there are two main ways in which you can do this:

One, through a futures contract.

And two, through an ETF.

When you purchase futures contracts on oil, you are basically purchasing oil production three months in advance. If you are not actually an oil refiner, you really won't have any need to take physical delivery of the oil.

So, when you purchase a futures contract, you can then sell the contract for a premium on the price you paid. This will entitle you to a profit as a seller while the buyer may benefit from paying a lower price on oil.

The other type of way you can invest in oil is through an ETF.

An oil ETF is a pool of money grouped together and invested in oil. Generally speaking, the funds raised through oil ETFs will be most likely invested in oil futures. Since investors in oil ETFs want exposure to the commodity but are unconcerned about taking physical delivery of the commodity, you can earn interest on your investment in the ETF.

This is a great way for you to earn some passive income while having the option of selling your stake in the ETF and making some cash on the sale of your position.

Investing in commodities may end up providing you with a great opportunity to play off a longer-term trend in which prices are rising.

What about Forex?

Forex is another great opportunity for you to engage in position trading.

Since Forex pits currency combinations against one another, fluctuations are certain to be plentiful.

As such, short-term fluctuations in Forex markets can wreak havoc on the sanity of day traders.

For position traders, the longer-term approach may favor them particularly during times of economic downturn among countries.

For example, if you pair up the US Dollar versus the Euro, the trends observed in both the Dollar and the Euro may determine whether one currency will gain in value relative to the other.

This implies that if Europe enters some sort of economic downturn which puts pressure on their currency, you might consider betting against the Euro.

On the other hand, if the US Dollar Index is declining due to strong economies throughout the world, you might choose to bet against the Dollar and stock up on Euros.

Either way, short-term profits might be non-existent since the market fluctuations affect pennies on the dollar, at best. But if you consider a longer-term approach, you will be able to make much larger profits since swings in currency can take longer than anticipated.

Consequently, Forex traders can take advantage of the shift in the economic landscape of individual countries which end up reflected in their currency's valuation.

Bonds

Bonds are often overlooked when considering position trading.

Bonds provide excellent opportunities to allocate funds into safer investment vehicles which are also highly liquid. This means that investors can quickly liquidate their bonds and get cash whenever they need to.

Most importantly, bonds come in all shapes and sizes. For example, there are 3 and 6-month bonds and range all the way up to 30 years.

The shorter-term bonds provide excellent opportunities for investors to put some money into solid investments without tying up their money for too long.

As such, traders can hold their positions for longer periods of time while collecting interest payouts from bonds.

Long-term bonds such as 10-year ones may offer better returns in the long run but would be better suited for passive investors who wish to lock up their investments with very specific, long-term goals in mind such as retirement and paying for college education.

Precious Metals

Precious metals (gold, silver, platinum, and palladium) don't get a lot of love from day traders.

These metals are usually traded as commodities and can be traded either through futures or ETFs.

Investors who wish to gain exposure to precious metals may do so by buying into an ETF and riding out the long-term waves that come with these commodities.

In general, investors tend to seek out precious metals when currencies such as the Dollar take a downturn or if other commodities such as oil, show considerable fluctuations.

As such, investors may look toward precious metals as a means of riding out longer periods of volatility. Nevertheless, day traders tend to shy away from precious metals and industrial metals, such as copper and aluminum since they offer very little regarding gains in the short term.

For an investor to make considerable gains from investing in metals, they would need to hold onto their positions for extended periods of months, at least several months, or even years, before they could see the true benefit of investing in this type of asset class.

Index Funds

Index funds are funds which don't invest in individual stocks, but rather invest in a collective approach following a major stock index. For instance, an index fund pegged to the Dow Jones would contain a stock of several companies traded on the Dow.

This would ensure exposure to several individual stocks while providing a greater degree of diversification in the types of stocks themselves.

As such, traders may choose to hold on to these funds for months at a time, especially when the markets are bullish.

Index funds provide decent returns and reduce risk considerably as fluctuations in individual stocks can be offset by the fluctuations in others. Therefore, if one stock falls, and others rise, this offsetting function will allow the investor to gain by the market's overall trend.

Index funds are also highly liquid, especially in times of consistent market gains. When markets are booming, index funds gain quite a bit of popularity from average investors and day traders alike.

Investing in index funds may also be a part of a more conservative investment approach since investors and traders will only lose money if the markets, as a whole, tank in unison. This can happen in times of economic shocks and devastating events, such as 9/11. Barring anything like 9/11, markets remain relatively steady, and investors can generally decipher the overall market trends.

Final Thoughts on Position Trading

I would encourage you to take a closer look at position trading especially if you are looking for a less trade-intensive approach. Since fees and commissions can add up, you can look to the types of investments which won't require you to engage in high-frequency trading.

Also, there is an important benefit that can be derived from position trading: passive income.

If you play your cards right, you can generate a decent amount of passive income just by making a series of trades at specific points in time. Since you won't be required to be at your desk at all times, you can hang back somewhat and let your investments do the work for you.

One word of caution though: when you are a position trader, you cannot take your eyes off the ball. If you do, you might miss changes in economic and market conditions which may adversely affect your portfolio. When that happens, you might sustain losses before you are able to react accordingly.

So, even if you are not keen on making a large number of trades, you still need to make sure you don't miss what's going on in financial markets.

VALUE INVESTING

Value investing is another useful tool you can have at your disposal.

In short, value investing can be defined as those stocks whose market value is below their book value.

To get fully understand how this strategy works, let's start off by defining what book value is.

Book value refers to the accounting valuation of a stock.

As such, book value can be calculated in the following manner:

assets (-) liabilities = equity

This is the foundational equation in accounting, and it serves to determine a company's equity. Equity can be equated to a company's capital, that is, the company's real value. Next, you take the total equity and divide it by the number of outstanding shares, and you get the value of each share based on its equity, hence, its book value.

So, what is the difference then between book value and market value?

Well, book value, as has been stated, depends on the company's actual accounting practices to determine the amount corresponding to assets and then liabilities.

The information needed to calculate this value can be derived from all of the financial information that is generated as a result of a company's operations.

Market value, on the other hand, is what investors are willing to pay for that stock. Therefore, market value implies a much more psychological condition than a practical one.

Consequently, if a stock has solid financial fundamentals, then it is quite likely that investors will be willing to pay more than the stock's actual book value. Conversely, if a stock's financials don't reflect much potential for growth and expansion, then investors may choose to pay very little for it to a point where investors may end up paying less than that that stock's book value is.

Consider this example:

XYZ corporation has a book value of $10 a share. Since it has sound fundamentals and it is growing at a rapid rate, investors want to get in as much as possible. That implies that investors are willing to pay an increasing amount per share to get their hands on that stock. This means that the individual shares of XYZ corporation have a market value of $100. That's a $90 spread.

In this example, investors are well aware that the stock is on the rise and there will always be someone who is willing to pay more for it. So, the increased demand in the stock keeps pushing the price up. This has caused its market value to exceed its book value by a wide margin.

Now consider the opposite scenario.

XYZ corporation's shares have a book value of $10. However, the company has been going through some rough times lately, and its earnings have dropped, its market share has been reduced, and they have shown management issues. Consequently, investors have kept dumping the stock until its share price has reached $8 a share.

In this scenario, the company is in rough shape and investors have taken note. The fact that the share price on this stock is below its market value, the company may find itself is a tight squeeze.

But this isn't necessarily a bad thing.

You see, when a stock's market value is below its book value, you might consider how this company may have a potential for growth.

And that's where it gets very tricky.

To find the "hidden gems," much research and study need to be done as to why the company's market price has sunk so low.

Sometimes, there are strong companies that are just underperforming. They have sounds fundamentals and management, but they lack a leader with vision and initiative. So, the company's board may choose to hire a new CEO.

In other cases, some companies have been hit hard by changes in their industry such as technological advancements that have given competitors an edge.

Other times, companies are simply performing very poorly and may be on a downward spiral that may lead them to their demise.

This is why value investment requires you to understand why the company has been beaten up and if there is any chance the company can rebound. If it does, you can clean up when share prices come back up. If it doesn't, you can hope to make a modest profit at best.

Nevertheless, value investing can provide position traders with a golden opportunity to make very interesting deals. Since you would be speculating on the company rebounding after hard times, it would be hard to make a profit on it in a day trading approach.

To maximize return on it, you would have to take a position trading approach and hold on to the stock for a considerable amount of time. In that case, it may even take years before the stock finally rebounds and you are able to make a profit on it.

However, not all is lost.

Investors are always looking for deals. As such, undervalued companies may prove to be just that. There might be some steals out there with a tremendous upside. You can capitalize on these opportunities and then make a killing when other investors are seeking out good deals.

How to Approach Value Investing

The first thing I would encourage you to do is have a look at companies whose share prices you would consider to be low. For example, you could look at stocks that are valued at under $10 a share.

Another good source is the so-called penny stocks. These stocks have shares that are valued below a Dollar or have share prices in the single digits.

These stocks may provide some very interesting opportunities since they may be poised for a turnaround. That turnaround may lead to gains in its market price. This would enable shareholders to make some good profits down the road.

Next, keep your eyes and ears open for companies which are under restructuring, bankruptcy protection, changing their management teams, or in a rebuilding process. These companies may very well be undervalued and given their plans, may turn their ship around.

After, you can jump into the fray and take a position in this company.

Next is the tricky part.

How long do you wait until you see results?

Well, the first part to that answer is actually very easy: if you see that company's market value drop at any point, get rid of it. If it's a struggling company, and they are still bleeding, there will be nowhere to go but all the way down.

Otherwise, you can determine what amount of time you are comfortable waiting to see a turnaround. Perhaps one month? Two months? Three months?

It's really up to you.

However, I wouldn't hold on to an undervalued stock for an extended period of time unless I was actually seeing some improvement in the company's valuation.

Unless you see that the market price is rising, even if it's slow like molasses, you can feel confident in it. But if you don't see any kind of movement or even risk of it continuing to trend downward, you might end up getting stuck with worthless stock.

One other type of value investing tip that you might consider is investing in companies which might be bought out by other corporations.

When this happens, the company that is being bought out will usually get a fairly good deal from the larger corporation that is looking to make the takeover. This type of situation may lead you to get a good deal on your stock even if the market isn't warming up too much to it.

Often, larger corporations will buy up struggling firms because they want a brand name, patents, or other specific assets that, that company possesses. So, it's easier for a larger corporation just to buy up the entire company and not the individual brands or patents.

Again, this could be a chance for you to make some good returns. Although, as I have stated earlier, this type of investing requires a lot of time and effort in terms of research and study. But if you can develop a good skill at it, you could become very successful in this type of trading.

Final Considerations on Value Investing

There are always good deals out there. Often, these deals come from companies that have simply been going through a rough patch and need some work. This may come in the form of restructuring, turnover in management, or simply a fresh start.

When you find these companies, be sure to do your homework on them. If you find that they have sound fundamentals but have simply been going through a rough time, then you can bet on them turning things around.

But if you are looking at companies that have been struggling for a while and are on a downward slope into oblivion, then you might be better off staying away from it. You might only end up having to short sell your stock to others who may not even want it. That could potentially cost you big time.

RISK AND VOLATILITY

Understanding risk and volatility are two of the most important things to keep in mind with the stock market. In this chapter, we are going to cover the main types of risk that you need to be aware of when investing. We will also talk about ways to manage risk. Finally, we'll talk about volatility, which is a natural part of the stock market. Any investor in the stock market needs to understand volatility and be able to quantify it. Fortunately, it's pretty simple.

Risk

There are many different types of risk in the stock market. Some are direct, such as a small company that has the **potential** to make gains because of innovative products. Others are indirect and external. You can't manage all types of risks. Some come out of the blue, like the 9/11 terrorist attacks or the 2008 financial crash. So, if you think that you can control every form of risk, take a deep breath and realize you can't. In this chapter, we are going to try and describe every major category of risk investor face, and if possible, we'll suggest ways to deal with them.

Emotional and Person Risk

First and foremost, you can control the risks to your investments that come from personal factors. These include fear, impatience, and greed. Emotions like these can be hard to control, but learning to take charge of them is essential if you are going to be a successful investor. When real money is on the line, these emotions can become strong and overpowering. You must not let that happen.

The most common problem when it comes to emotions and personal risk is fear. When a stock market starts looking bearish, many investors immediately jump ship. They are making a huge mistake. A good investor is not getting in and out of the market at the slightest sign of a problem. In fact, selling off when everyone else is could be one of the biggest mistakes individual investors make. By the way, that doesn't exempt large investors. Many professional traders are subject to the same emotions and exhibit the same behavior during downturns. Massive selloffs are what cause bear markets to develop.

First of all, remember that you are looking to hold your investments over the long term. So ups and downs of the market and even recessions are not a reason to sell them. Over the past 50 years, by far the worst stock market contraction happened in the 2008 financial crisis. However, even that was short-lived. People that sold off their investments were either faced with being out of the markets altogether or having to get back in the markets when prices were appreciating. The lifetimes of other major bear markets were similar or even more short-lived. The first lesson in managing personal risk is to hold your investments through downturns.

The second lesson is that rather than giving into fear, you should start to see market downturns as opportunities. When prices are rapidly dropping due to a market sell-off, you should be buying shares. It's impossible to know where the bottom of a market is, and you shouldn't concern yourself with that. At any time that share prices are declining, it's an opportunity, and so you should be making regular stock purchases. In one year, two years, or five years down the road, on average, the stocks that you purchased in a downturn are going to be worth quite a bit more.

The second problem that arises as a part of personal risk is greed. Many people start seeing dollar signs when they begin investing. Having a get rich quick mentality is not compatible with successful investing. Your approach should be centered on slowly and steadily accumulating wealth and not making a quick buck. As you invest, you're going to be coming across claims that certain trades or stocks are the next best thing, but you're better off ignoring such claims. More often than not, they turn out to be false. The stock market is not a gambling casino, even though many people treat it that way. You can avoid succumbing to greed by maintaining a regular investment program and not being taken in by the temptation that you can profit from short-term swings or "penny stocks" that are going to supposedly take off.

Finally, there is the related problem of impatience. After the Great Depression, people developed a more reasonable and cautious approach to the stock market. They realized that you're not going to get rich in six months or a year. The idea of long-term investing became dominant.

Unfortunately, in recent years, this lesson seems to be getting lost. More people are behaving like traders rather than as investors. Far too many investors are being taken in by the seduction of being able to beat market returns. Instead of being impatient, you should realize that you're in it for the long haul. Rather than trying to make a few extra bucks now, you're seeking to build wealth.

Risk of Loss of Capital

Obviously, financial risk is something you face when investing. Theoretically, there is a chance that you will lose all the money you invest in the stock market. This can happen if you tie your fate to a small number of companies. Several well-known companies like Lumber Liquidators, Bear-Stearns, and GM have either had major problems or gone completely under. Investors may have lost large sums in the process. The way to deal with this is to avoid investing in a small number of companies.

You'll also want to pay attention to the types of companies you invest in. Putting all of your money into small cap stocks, for example, is probably a bad idea. So is putting all of your money into emerging markets, or into one sector of the stock market. Again, the key message is diversification. It's the way to protect you from financial risk.

Market and Economic Risk

Some factors are beyond your control, and the economy inevitably cycles through slowdowns and downturns. The market will cycle along with the economy, and also experiences crashes when the economy may be doing fine overall. This happened in 1987, for example.

Interest Rate Risk

Changing interest rates can impact the markets. Although this is a book about stock market investing, you should have some awareness of how bond markets work. You should also be aware that investor money can flow back and forth between bond and stock markets depending on conditions.

One thing that bond markets offer is the safety of capital, especially when we are talking about U.S. government bonds. When interest rates are high, U.S. government bonds (and other types of bonds, including corporate and municipal bonds) become very attractive.

Interest rate changes have risks for bond investors, however. Bonds are traded on secondary markets. When interest rates rise, bond prices fall, because older bonds that offer lower interest rates become less attractive. Conversely, when interest rates fall, older bonds that pay higher interest rates have more value than new bonds being issued that pay relatively low rates.

This doesn't directly affect a stock market investor, but if demand for bonds rises, that can mean less capital flowing into the stock market. Less demand means lower prices, so the market may see declines.

Also, as we'll see, you can invest in bonds through the stock market using exchange-traded funds. If you are using this method, you'll want to keep close tabs on interest rates. That means paying closer attention to the Federal Reserve and their quarterly announcements. You should be doing so even if you are not going to invest in bonds in any way. Announcements on interest rate changes can have a large impact on stock prices. But as always, keep your eye on the long ball. If the markets react negatively to an increase in interest rates that can be an opportunity to buy undervalued stocks.

Political Risk and Government

Government and politics can create big risks in the stock market. International events can cause market crashes, and these days even a tweet from the President can cause markets to rise and fall. Lately, some politicians have also been discussing breaking up the big tech companies. Others are talking about investigating them. Such talk – and worse actions – can have a negative impact on the markets. Part of your job as an investor is to keep a close eye on the news. You're going to want to know what's happening so that you can adjust if necessary.

Inflation Risk

Inflation hasn't been high in decades. However, in the late 1970s inflation rates were routinely in the double digits.

Hopefully, that isn't going to be something that happens anytime soon, because high inflation rates can eat your returns alive. If the stock market is appreciating at 7% per year, but inflation is 14%, you can see that it's like having debt but investing in stocks – it's a losing proposition. Right now, inflation risk is very low, but you'll want to have some awareness of it and always keep tabs on it. High inflation rates also tend to go hand-in-hand with high-interest rates, since the Federal Reserve will raise rates to try and slow down inflation. That means that bonds might become more attractive when inflation gets out of control.

Taxes and Commissions

Finally, we have the risk imposed by taxes. Of course, we are all going to be hit with taxes no matter where our money comes from. However, you need to take into account the taxes that you are going to pay when it comes to any gains you realize on the stock market. Part of being a successful investor is having an understanding of how much your taxes are cutting into your profits. If you are investing for the long-term, it will be less of an issue. But keep in mind that taxes can really eat into short-term trades. Frequent, short-term traders also face risk from commissions and fees. If you execute a lot of trades, the commissions can add up. This is not an issue for long-term investors.

Risk vs. Return

One of the fundamental trade-offs that an investor will make is a risk vs. return. Generally speaking, the higher the risk, the greater the **possibility** of good returns. In 1998, Amazon was a pretty high-risk investment. While it had potential, major bookstores like Borders and Barnes & Noble dominated the space. Amazon was on shaky ground at the time, and another company could have come in and competed successfully for online book sales. That never happened, and Amazon ended up dominating book sales and expanding widely across retail and into cloud computing. That risk has translated into massive returns. A $10,000 investment in 1998 would be worth more than $1 million today.

But hindsight is 20/20. Today, there are similar opportunities all around us, but it's hard to know which ones are going to end up being successful over the long term. If you are an aggressive investor, part of your job is going to be estimating which companies are the best bets for the future.

Risk vs. return also plays a role in emerging markets. These countries may experience massive GDP growth year after year since they have lots of room to grow. Domestic companies that are growing with their economies can offer remarkable returns. However, there are many risks. Rapid growth can often evaporate with major downturns. Stability is lower in emerging markets; you could face complete loss of capital.

These examples serve to illustrate why a diversified portfolio is essential.

Managing Risk

There are a few time-tested strategies that have been developed that help manage risk. They even minimize, as much as possible, the kinds of risk that you will face that are completely out of control. That could include anything from a terrorist attack to interest rate changes.

These strategies are simple and easy to understand. The problem is that in practice, many investors fail to follow them, and instead let their decision making be guided by emotions. You might end up following that path as well. However, we are going to give you the tools you need to avoid it. It's up to you whether you utilize them or not.

Dollar Cost Averaging

The first strategy seeks to avoid being impacted by the ups and downs of the market. You don't know when you are buying at the top of a market or the bottom. None of us has a crystal ball, but what we can do is average out our investments over the long-term. You can do this using a technique called dollar cost averaging, which is simply buying shares at regular intervals – completely ignoring price fluctuations. Most ups and downs in the stock market are actually noise. So you should avoid worrying about them as much as possible. And we've already noted that stock goes up and down with bull and bear markets. Using dollar cost averaging, you remove the stress (and hence the emotion) that is associated with these fluctuations. The costs are averaged out because sometimes you are going to be buying when prices are low, even though at other times you will be buying when prices are relatively high.

Speaking of rising share prices, this technique also helps you avoid another emotional problem. If share prices are rising, many investors panic. The reason they panic is they are worried that share prices will rise to new heights and never come back down again. They will "miss an opportunity" of gains, and also be forced into a position of having to buy shares at higher prices.

Those short-term ups and downs don't matter over the long-term. Whether Amazon had a long gain 4 years ago or not won't matter to the investor using dollar cost averaging. All that matters is the long-term trend – and regularly purchasing shares along the way. Looking at the chart below, we've used an arrow to show Amazon's long-term trend and circled a few of the short-term fluctuations that at the time, caused a great deal of angst and anxiety. Traders probably tried to profit from them. But look how small they are, compared to the overall picture.

Diversification

A lot of people don't like to hear about this one since financial advisors are constantly shoving it down people's throats. But diversification remains one of the most important strategies in stock market investing. The problem is most investors don't diversify enough.

Having investments in 5-7 or even ten companies is not true diversification. When it comes to individual companies, having investments in 15-20 companies is probably the range you want to shoot for. The problem with investing in individual companies is that you have to strike a balance. On the one hand, you want to invest in a wide range of companies to lower risk, in case one or more of them take a tumble. On the other hand, as an individual investor, you also need to closely study the companies you invest in. There simply isn't time for one individual to closely study dozens of companies and keep up with them as time goes on. So twenty companies is considered the maximum limit for individual investors.

However, you should take things a step further. First of all, you need to look at sectors, not just companies. If you invest in twenty social media companies, you aren't diversified. The sector itself could take a hit, causing all the companies in the sector to go into a tailspin. When they do, your investments sink with the sector.

The best way to diversify your portfolio is to utilize fund investing. Mutual funds aren't a personal favorite, but you can use them as part of an overall strategy if you would like to. Most individual investors are interested in a more active role in their portfolios, so don't typically do that.

Instead, you should consider using exchange-traded funds. They trade like stocks and give you a large amount of diverse exposure.

Volatility

The next topic we are going to address in this chapter is volatility. You probably have an intuitive understanding of what this means. Graphically, it's represented by the jagged appearance of stock market charts. Prices are moving up and down, dramatically swinging between highs and lows. That's what volatility is. It can be measured in terms of the frequency of price changes and the magnitude. The higher the differences between the highs and lows, and the more frequently stock prices fluctuate, the higher the volatility.

Traders like high volatility. That means there are more opportunities for stock prices to trend in their favor. An options trader, for example, likes a high volatility stock because, over the lifetime of the option, the probability is increased that the share price will move to a favorable position, even if it's just for a short time.

Conservative investors either don't like volatility or if the fundamentals are good, they don't care about it. The thing about volatility is that it's usually a short-term measure. For example, Amazon has a high level of volatility. But does that matter to a long-term investor? Not really. The overall trend within which that volatility is taking place is what matters.

For a long-term investor, worrying about volatility is something that should be occupying a relatively low position on your list. And by long-term, we mean anything more than a 1-year time frame. Consider Microsoft, which has relatively low volatility, much less than Amazon. Looking at its five-year chart, it has a similar trend. So did the volatility matter?

To quantify the volatility of a stock, you will want to take a look at a quantity investors call **Beta**. This compares the volatility of any given stock to the entire market. The volatility of the market is 1.0. Any number above this indicates that the stock is more volatile than the market. Any number below this indicates that the stock is less volatile than the market.

Amazon has a beta of 1.75. That means its 75% more volatile than the market (note these numbers are subject to change). Microsoft has a volatility of 1.05. That means it's slightly more volatile than the market – 5 % more. However, it's much less volatile than Amazon.

General Electric has a volatility of 0.90. That's a low volatility stock. It's 10% less volatile as the entire market. But does that make it attractive? Probably not – the share price is only 1/3 what it was just a few years ago.

Volatility can also be negative. If volatility is positive, that means the share price tends to rise when the overall stock market rises. And when stock prices fall, the market is probably falling as well. Amazon and Microsoft both rise and fall, on average, with the overall market.

If volatility is negative, that means that on average, the stock moves against the market. So when share prices are rising, the stock market is declining, and vice versa.

Volatility has been rising. But that isn't necessarily something to be afraid of. One of the reasons that it's rising is technology. Since it's easier to place trades, decisions by large investors that can buy and sell massive amounts of shares quickly can cause stock prices to fluctuate by larger amounts over shorter time periods. It's also a lot easier for individual investors and traders to make moves on the market. While as an individual, you practically have zero influence, when you sum up the decisions of large numbers of investors that fit together in herd behavior, this can have an impact as well.

COMMON MISTAKES AND HOW TO AVOID THEM

Relying on Emotions

M ost people lose on the stock market because they cannot manage their emotions.

It is proven that small savers buy in the upward phase of the markets, and panic sells at the first sign of decrease. Then what happens is that the market recovers, and they are now out.

This happens because of the poor financial education of the average American investor.

He, who does not know how to assess the risk and the diversification, cannot select the securities to put in the portfolio. He does not know how to calculate the average value of an asset. He does not even know how to use a spreadsheet to calculate the volatility of a stock. And, it is precisely the lack of ability to manage the risk that will make him resort to bad decisions which, will ultimately result in a loss.

Speculating, Not Investing

Another mistake that many often make is to confuse speculating with investing.

If you invest for the very short term, you increase the risk, and it is not a question of investment but of speculation. Knowing how to define investment speculation is essential.

Before entering a title, you must define your time horizon and consider where to put the stop loss. One classical example of speculation is "binary options." They are often promoted as an investment, but they are really not. For those who do not know what they are, binary options are bets placed on the price of an asset in the next 30 seconds. Yes, you read that right. Seriously, stay away from them.

Investing without Planning

On the stock market, invested capital should not be necessary for daily life. Before investing, plan these goals. Someone invests because he wants to buy a bigger house in the future. Others may invest for when they retire, but also for a holiday. There are those who do it for their children.

The real question is… "Why are you investing?"

Thinking to Be Able to Predict the Future

What do Warren Buffet from Omaha and life coach Tony Robbins have in common? Both agree on the big risk that comes when our money is at stake.

During an interview with CNBC, Tony Robbins warned against a big mistake that is committed when it comes to investing for the future, which is, trying to predict the ups and downs of the market.

No one can predict the future, says Robbins, and legendary investors like billionaire Warren Buffett and the founder of the titanic hedge fund Bridgewater Associates, Ray Dalio, tend to agree.

"Your plan for the future cannot be based on trying to time the market because you're going the wrong way."

Instead of buying and selling shares based on how the small change, Robbins suggests thinking long-term.

"You cannot afford to try and time the market. What we must do is study the long-term elements, and have a diversification plan that protects when we are wrong."

Buffett is also an important supporter of this type of strategy called "buy and hold," so much so that he wagered that the S & P 500 stock index would surpass hedge funds (which actively change investments). Now, it seems that most likely he will win that bet, which will bring him an extra $2 million in prize money.

Robbins also relies on the advice of Dalio, who founded the largest hedge fund in the world, Bridgewater Associates, which has difficulty identifying the right times to get in and out of investments. So, for Robbins, the best idea remains to look long-term, and both he and Buffett suggest that they consider investing in low-cost index funds as the best thing to do.

Not Paying Attention to Costs

We have said it in all languages: costs can kill you financially. Investing $15,000 for 30 years can result in $106,000 capital if made with an ETF or a low-cost mutual fund, and $67,000 if it is carried out with a mutual fund that has 2% of TER. See it for yourself.

Realistically, saving costs is the only true "free money" that you can get as an investor. Financial products with high commissions are more often than not skylarks; just think of how overestimated Alfa management's idea is.

Changing the Duration of the Investment "On the Go"

It usually works like this: you have chosen a portfolio assuming a certain duration of the investment, then the market "coughs," an instrument within the portfolio loses 5-6%, you read some negative opinions about it, start to shake like a rabbit, and eventually sell. This change of time horizon does monstrous damages. It normally makes you lose about half of the gains. Solution: invest a little at a time and do not think about it anymore.

Not Diversifying

Diversification is useless only if you are able to predict the future and know what the best investment will be. If instead (as a normal human being) you do not have paranormal divinatory skills, you should diversify your portfolio a little without exaggerating (more on that later).

Doing Everything Your Broker Says

If the bank, the promoter, or the broker pushes a product, run to check the costs: in 9 out of 10 cases, it is the most convenient product for them and, as you can guess, the most expensive for you.

Not Reading Prospectuses and Contracts Well

By law, intermediaries are forced to write everything they do in a "contract" type of document. Often times, they will do it with that legal language that sends you into narcosis already in the second line. Hence you have to read everything if you do not want bad surprises. Remember that you are responsible for your money and should not put the blame on others.

Buying Unit-linked (and Index-linked) Policies

These policies are among the less transparent financial products that can be found and are padded with high commissions in favor of those who sell them. The seller will tell you a lot of nice stories about the capital guarantee.

With a unit-linked (or index-linked) policy, nine out of 10 chances you will have an expensive product with severe penalties in case of early disinvestment and, after 10 or 20 years of payments, you will typically be rewarded with a disappointing performance (but, if you can console yourself, you will have made the man who sold it to you very happy).

Buying Bonds from Your Bank

Bank bonds usually make less of a BTP of the same maturity, because they bear implicit charges, like costs for example. Then, they are on average riskier and less liquid. This is even more true for subordinated bank bonds, whose holders, with the recent entry into force of the bail-in, are likely to be called to put their hands in the portfolio in the event of the issuer's default. Before buying these bonds, study them carefully, compare them with a governmental or supranational title (like BEI, BIS, etc.), and only then decide.

Believing to Get Rich with Online Trading

The colorful world of online trading is teeming with gurus to convince you that you will become rich, thanks to their fabulous courses or their financial market forecasting site. Know that succeeding with trading is very difficult: in the vast majority of cases, you will end up losing money and time. Learn to save and invest, not to trade.

Listening to Economists, Politicians and Mass Media

The noise in the ears distracts: eliminate it. So here is, for you and only for you, our personal list of noises that you have to get rid of.

- **Economists.** Think about how little they have put us right in the story: for example, in 2009, they did not recognize the worst crisis since the Great Depression of 1929 in spite of a myriad of signals and, above all, the fact that the recession was already under its way.

- **Politicians.** Except for rare exceptions, the events of any Parliament are lively, full of funny and quarrelsome characters that combine all the colors, going from crisis to sudden solutions, and then plunge again into tragic crises: perfect plots for journalistic-television sagas. Generally, the impact on the financial markets of all this is low.

For example, despite the ups and downs of Italian politics, the spread has continued on its way, indifferent to everything but the ECB. Going on historical facts of weight, think that after the Japanese attack on Pearl Harbor in 1941 (which dragged the US into World War II), the stock index Dow Jones only lost 6% (and in the following 12 months it gained 2,20%).

- **Mass media:** newspapers, television. They bombard you with a continuous stream of news and data (often superficially explained) which lead you to deviate from your investment path (see point 2). Every day, some economic data comes out: sometimes they improve, sometimes they get worse, but, in the immediate future, they rarely impact on your investments. Just to say, during the last recession in the Eurozone (which began in March 2012 and ended in June 2013), Eurozone stock markets have gained about 13%. So, you focus on a few important things: check your wallet regularly, follow the right source of information, but do not be paranoid about the news.

Wanting to Become Successful Overnight

Do not be the investor who wants immediate success and who loses patience for daily highs and lows. Wanting quick results is certainly an example of how not to invest your savings if you want to succeed.

Investing successfully is a bit like taking care of a vegetable garden. Plants grow slowly, with the first few years bearing little fruits, but then start to grow faster. In general, it is foolish to expect significant results in a few weeks, months or even in a few years. Remember that you do not want to get rich fast, you want to get rich for sure.

Not Taking Profits

It may seem strange, but there are lots of investors that never take out their profits. This is detrimental since they never enjoy the money they earned with investing. It is like getting a gym subscription, but never going to the gym: it is useless and does not bring back to the practice.

The most successful investors always take out profits from time to time. Obviously, we are talking about calculated decisions and planned moves. However, the gold nugget here is the fact that if you do not have the money in your bank account, you cannot actually use it. It may sound silly, but it is a fact that most beginners tend to forget.

UNDERSTANDING OPTIONS

The big question is: how do you apply your skills to make money on the stock market? Before you finish reading this book, you will get some answers. You need to see the patterns and setups as they appear, not just after that - anyone can see them afterward. This is followed by a possible application method. Rules are created. Charts show patterns and the locations where the rules for determining entry and exit points should be applied.

Determine whether the congestion is a re-accumulation or re-distribution based on the last increase or break. Assume this until the congestion pattern tells you otherwise.

The Stop

We propose two steps: an average spread below the last reaction low or the span of the entry bar below the entry bar. Once we have some freedom of movement, the stop will be tightened. Close the position if the price does not behave within three bars. Then do not wait until the stop is triggered.

Trade or Not?

You do not risk your capital if you are not invested in the market. This trading style limits exposure to approximately 10% to 15% of the total observation period. Between 85% and 90% of the time, you are not in the market. During an accumulation or distribution phase, a position can be held. Although there is nothing wrong with this approach, it involves the risk of losing significant portions of the profits. The pattern may be distribution rather than accumulation. You need to study many charts until you find that this approach is workable and fits your trading style. This approach requires a lot of judgment. They should try to automate as many rules as possible to minimize uncertainty.

Trade High-Value Assets

Active trading is best suited for the stocks and/or futures that are moving or in trend phases, and not the boring ones like the securities that are constantly going sideways. The definition of a value that moves is quite subjective. Many sources cite lists of securities that outperform and outperform others, and one of the best is Investor's Business Daily.

Moving securities may have the following characteristics:

- Increased volatility
- Reaching a new four-week high
- Securities in the rising phase
- Significantly upwards or downwards inclined sliding average of the last 20 days
- The leading values in a specific market segment

Brief Summary

Remember, the goal of this game is to win, not that you're in 90% of all price moves. Open your positions when certain patterns occur and realize your profits when the target price is reached or at the first sign that the offer exceeds demand.

These basic principles apply to every time horizon, including day trading. If you are long-term oriented, use weekly charts. This will lead to many false signals, but there are indeed the stops. You will only earn money by studying countless charts and drawing your entry points, exit points, and stop loss. Thereby you internalize these approaches and make them suitable. After that, you could succeed in trading. One of the hardest things in trading is closing a position towards the end of an outbreak or during a buying spike. Just tell yourself that you are a nice person: everyone wants to have the stock, and you give yours.

The General Motors study might be one example of how you can create a supply-demand based trade system. Create two charts: one shows what you should have done and the other what you really did. Learn by comparison. Recognize the forces that act at important turning points.

Practical Application of the Elliott Wave Theory

The Elliott Wave Theory confuses many traders. In this chapter, we do not want to discuss the ambiguity of this theory, but we apply it to a trading plan that should develop into a successful approach. This theory is one of the best theories of the Cycle because it allows non-harmonic movements.

There are many different approaches to securities trading. These are roughly divided into fundamental and technical approaches. Some technicians like to mix both methods for an optimal market approach. The fundamental access includes bushels, hectares, consumption units, revenues, book values and so on. Technical Analysis examines past price movements and predicts future ones. In 1939, Elliott published a series of articles describing the principle of Elliott waves. The Elliott Wave Theory is one of the best technical methods for market analysis, and the serious-interested should certainly include it in his studies.

Is it possible to predict price trends using the Elliott Wave Theory and use this information profitably? The answer to that is a cautious yes if you do not make the theory an exact science. The Elliott Wave Theory allows harmonic and non-harmonic course movements. Most cycle theories use principles based on harmonic movements. As soon as nonharmonic movements occur, it becomes difficult.

The following summary of the Elliott Wave Theory reduces the ideas to a useful size:

1. Ascending moves consist of five waves, two of which are corrections. Falling movements are counterproductive. The odd waves run in the direction of the main motion. Straight waves run against the main direction. Shaft 2 corrects shaft 1. Shaft 5 corrects shaft 4. Sometimes there are nine or more waves. Elliott solves this problem by calling these movement extensions.

2. The endpoint of shaft 4 is higher than the height of shaft 1. Elliott specifies lengths proportions exactly, such as that the shaft 4 should be shorter than the waves 3 and 5. However, it has been found that this is not necessarily true.

The movements are divided into waves that are one degree smaller. What does "one degree smaller" mean? This question is difficult to answer, and that is one of the reasons why applying the theory is so difficult. One suggestion is to look for it in the next shorter timeframe. If you have a daily chart, look for the smaller grade on a 30-minute chart. The next smaller degree also needs five waves to complete the higher-order wave 1 and is therefore identical to the daily chart.

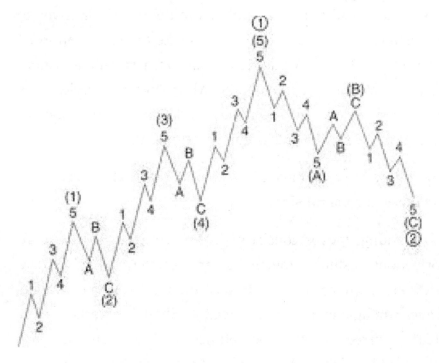

Triangular Corrections

Triangular corrections consist of a five-point pattern (ABCDE) after a thrust. The type and position of such a pattern often allow conclusions to be drawn as to whether a turnaround is pending or not.

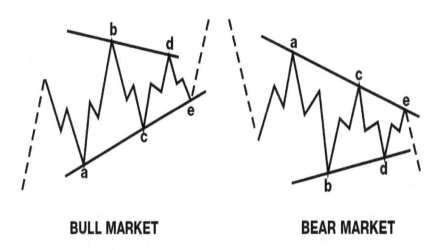

BULL MARKET   **BEAR MARKET**

A-Shaped Corrections

The length and duration of the first correction wave or A-shaped correction of the thrust are of utmost importance for determining the further course of the total correction and the probability of a turnaround.

Look for the application of the A-wave (the first correction wave to increase) to determine the type of correction and the probable direction of the price after the correction has been completed. Then, you can see four possible price movements. If the extent of the A correction wave is the same, the following should be deduced:

- 25% - 35%: Indicates a single correction wave.

- 35% - 50%: Indicates a three-wave correction.

- 50% - 75%: Indicates a five-wave correction.

- Over 75%: mostly a possible trend reversal.

Prediction of the Corrections

This type of price development can lead to a turnaround. Here are the forces of supply and demand at work. A reaction at a distance of 75% from the starting point makes a clearer statement than a low-25% reaction.

Understanding Options Terminology

For logical reasons, the option's duration is a factor. If you'll like an asset to be controlled for five years rather than one year, normally, having it controlled for a longer period of time would cost more. Alternately, it would not cost as much, in the event that you needed the asset controlled for just one day,

This is because the more the asset is being controlled, the more likely it is that something can happen (there's that word again) to affect its price. If for example, the property was controlled for just one day, it isn't too likely that a major real estate bargain involving your property will be reported that day.

OPTIONS RISK AND REWARD

Money management is only included in the trading plan by about one-tenth of all private traders. Just because a trader does not have a lot of capital does not mean that he cannot apply the principles of money management. Many traders are of the opinion that these ideas can only be used by large asset managers and institutions.

Money management also implies that the potential risk, taking into account the preferences of the trader, is set in relation to the expected profit. The goal is to set a desirable yield rate and then minimize the associated risk. Trading generally requires four decisions:

1. Buy/sell (system or strategy)?
2. Which security is traded?
3. How many contracts or shares of value are traded?
4. What is the share of capital risked on a trade?

The first decision is about the trading process itself without taking into account money management. The other three decisions involve maximizing profit and minimizing risk directly. The foundations of risk and reward should be considered from the start in the development of a trading system and must become an integral part of the system.

If a trader works profitably right from the start and has thus increased his trading capital, then he cannot be ruined by four losses (as long as his bet remains the same). Although the number of consecutive losses that would lead to ruin increases with time, so does the likelihood of multiple losses following one another. The following formula calculates the probability of ultimate ruin (WR) over time:

WR = (1-VT / 1 + VT) AH

VT stands for the trader's advantage (percentage winners - percent losers), and AH is the initial trading units. If the initial capital of a trader is $ 20,000 and his bet per trade is $ 5,000 then AH = 4. The following example calculates the probability of ultimate ruin:

- Total Capital§ 20,000Total Capital$ 20,000
- Deployment$ 5,000Deployment§ 2,500
- Advantage of the Trade10%Trades' Advantage10%
- Chance of Ruin44.8%Chance of Ruin20.1%
- Total Capital$ 20,000Total Capital$ 20,000
- Bet$ 2,000Bet$ 1,000
- Advantage of the Trade10%Advantage of the Trade10%
- Chance of Ruin13.4%Chance of Ruin1.8%

These numbers apply only when you trade one contract at a time. With changing contract numbers, the risk of ruin changes dramatically. Moreover, these calculations assume that, in the case of a profit, the amount is always the same and corresponds to the loss in the negative case. As mentioned above, the risk of ruin is determined by the percentage of winners, the ratio between winners and losers, and the size of the bet. So far, we have disregarded the relationship between winners and losers. In real life, most successful trading systems score less than 50% winners and win-loss ratios above 1.2.

The risk of ruin is an interesting indicator, but it does not give much insight into how to use or manage capital efficiently. For self-preservation, it is best not to put everything on one card. If you choose your bets well and follow a system with a positive bias, the risk of ruin is very low.

The Capital Allocation Model

Now you know the tools you need to understand our capital allocation model. First, we'll show how capital is allocated to a one-market portfolio using a small selection of data. Later, we will apply the same approach to a two-market portfolio. As you know, our goal is to maximize profit while minimizing risk. This goal must be achieved without exceeding the limits of justifiable risk. To reach the goal, we need to know how much capital is to be allocated to each market and what number of contracts should be traded. In this model, capital is calculated from the market value of the account, the average monthly returns, and the market risk. The market value is simply the starting capital with which we begin our trading. In these examples, the returns do not add up; we use the initial capital for all calculations. The average monthly income is the capital that we can expect to gain from our system. Market risk is the amount we can lose per day on a trade. Asset managers use a variety of metrics to assess market risk:

• Mean Range: The average of the ranges of the last three to 50 Days, which is converted into a monetary amount in US $. For example, if the average spread is 40 points for the Swiss franc over the past 10 days and the Swiss franc is $ 12.50, the market risk is $ 500. The likely amount of market movement is the average spread of the last x days. This does not always have to be right, but the capital allocation model needs to be built on certain probabilities.

•The average change in closing prices: The average change in closing prices over the last three to 50 days says more about the risk, as this value indicates the expected risk if the position is held.

•Mean change in positive closing prices versus negative closing prices: the average change in the negative closing prices over a period suggests the risk of holding a long position.

• The standard deviation of closing prices: The standard deviation of the closing prices gives a more accurate picture of the risk, as the daily deviation is displayed with a probability of 68%. This calculation is a bit more complex, but it does not cause any problems with the computers available today.

In whatever way we measure the risk, it is the most important variable to watch and the most important component of the capital allocation model.

A Market Portfolio

Whether the system trades futures or stocks makes no difference. Before we can allocate capital, the average monthly income and market risk must be determined on the basis of a contract. We also need to determine how much of our capital we are willing to risk per trade. But we cannot know that yet, because that's exactly what we want to find out.

Cumulating of Results

Cumulating means here the process of capital allocation based on the current portfolio or deposit value. The current portfolio value results from the start-up capital as well as the already completed positive and negative trades. When it comes to large sums of money, accumulation is very good: the capital invested increases or decreases depending on the current value of the deposit. If a trading plan is successful, then each trade will be given more capital; but if it is bad, then there is less capital available for each trade. Note that we have found that cumulating is very good when it comes to large sums. This limitation stems from the belief that the allocation should not be extended until the seed capital of smaller accounts has not been at least doubled or tripled. Even good systems can crash after a series of wins, and if a smaller account does not cumulate, there is still some capital left for bad times. If accumulation is of interest to you (and it should, if you have significant sums of money), then you can build it into the capital allocation model with a small change. In the formula, do not use seed capital as total capital (GK), but use the current value of the deposit.

PENNY STOCK STRATEGIES

Find a Penny Stock with Future Value: The value of penny stocks increases and decreases with no real guarantees, which means that when you calculate a penny stock's future value, you are calculating your desired or anticipated return and it is not something that you can necessarily count on. However, when you calculate your expected return, you get an idea of whether or not it may be worth the risk of purchasing it.

In order to find a company with future value, start by examining that company's five-year history, when available. Many companies that issue penny stocks are usually fairly new businesses, so acquiring a history can be difficult. Keep in mind that you can also research a new company by researching its owner(s), partners, and/or investors. You can use a timeline longer than five years if you wish, but make sure not to use less than a five year history. You then will take each year's starting price per share and subtract the end of the year price per share. Now you will average out these numbers by adding them together and then dividing that sum by five. This is the dividend data for your stock.

The formula for an expected return is:

• R = (Dividends paid + Capital gains)/price of stock

•This formula states that your Return, or R, is equal to the sum of the dividends paid, which is your dividend data, and the capital gains, which the difference of what you would have paid at the beginning of the year for a stock and what you would have made if you sold the stock at the end of the year, divided by the price of the stock

This formula will give you your average yearly expected return percentage based on the company's historic data that you have researched. There are also various return calculators that you can use on the internet.

Focus on liquidity: While liquidity is always a concern when investing in a securities market, there are few places where it will more drastically come into play than when you are dealing with penny stocks no matter the exchange, specifically if you are planning to practice day trading. Liquidity can be thought of as a function of spread which, in turn, can be thought of like the difference between what the stock is currently selling for and what it is currently being purchased for or is estimated to be selling for at a point in the future.

This difference stems from the fact that a majority of the stock that is bought or sold each day is sold by brokerages rather than individuals or the companies themselves which means that the rate at which the stock is sold can vary dramatically, even in a particularly short period of time. As a rule, the greater the spread, the more difficulty you will have moving the stock in question when the time comes to do something with it besides just hang on and hope for the best. When you are working with penny stocks you are in the relatively unique position in that the spread you are looking at can sometimes get to the point where there is practically no way you can ever expect to sell the stock in question.

While holding on to a penny stock when it is on a strong upswing can be tempting, the right move here is to sell after you have seen enough positive movement to make it worth your while as it is likely not a question of if the stock is going to turn back around but when. Selling from a reasonable point on the spectrum will allow you to avoid the problems that might develop if the spread gets too large.

Strategy 18 -Profit From The Rise, Never The Fall: Sure you know to buy low and sell high, but invariability you will come across someone spouting the idea that short selling a penny stock is a great way to turn a profit. Yes, it is conceivable that you can make money by short selling a penny stock that has seen lots of activity, but the risks far outweigh the rewards here. Short selling a stock is not as simple as selling options on a stock. It requires enough capital to fulfill the short sell should the stock price go in the opposite direction. It is both hard to fill these orders and to get them approved by a brokerage firm.

You are likely to spend more time actually trying to short sell a stock successfully than actually being able to commit to the short. In addition, the upside to short selling is when you identify a company that is overvalued. Since the underlying financial reports and asset lists of each of these companies are so dubious, it's naïve to think that you will be able to pick the right company to short sell. It's different than investing in a company that you believe in; you must actively believe that a company will fail and know that other investors will carry out this failure through selling the stock - two things that are so hard to predict and come with so much risk that you should just never go this route.

Strategy 19 -How to Find a Penny Stock Before it Spikes: It is fairly important for a penny stock trader to be able to tell when a stock is spiking. Of course, there is no 100% guarantee that will let you know what every single stock will be doing in every single situation – this is the stock market after all - but there are several signals that you may use in order to try and predict when spikes will occur.

Bet on a stock's price action. Many potential investors make the mistake of attempting to predict when a spike is occurring by paying a visit to their chatroom of choice to check in with other members to see what stocks they think may be moving or to see how high they think a specific stock is going to go. Other potential investors may buy alerts from a guru of sorts who may tell them when they should buy, according to their predicted spikes.

Seek out stocks that have a potential for breakouts that are reaching new highs. As a penny stock investor, it may behoove you greatly to always be keeping an eye out for those stocks that may be following this trend. This is especially true of those stocks that are holding the morning high and still up on the day. You do have to exercise some caution here though.

You can 'piggyback' on a stock that has spiked a bit already. Out of these four strategies, this one will certainly take up a lot less of your time than the others. Piggybacking is where an investor finds a stock that is already on its way up and is really one of the fastest methods of identifying a stock that is about to spike. There are plenty of research tools available online that can help investors to find this information. All you have to do is utilize them.

Strategy 20 -First-Hour Trading: In reality, the market is only trends throughout the entire day some 20 percent of the time. This means that, despite what you may think, most of the time the market is actually quite dull. The only time that this is not the case is when a large volume of sharp moves happen which is the first hour of every day.

Many traders prefer the 5-minute chart as in this amount of time you get plenty of volume and price spikes as the gap between the close of the previous day and this morning's opening becomes apparent. What's more, if you are on top of the news from the day you can likely get an idea of where the market will be going which means you won't be starting the day blind.

It is important to understand that this period is also the most volatile with an unstable range and few clear boundaries. Even with a system in place, the idea that a candlestick will play out as expected is still a gamble in this stage rather than a sure thing. If you are looking to get serious about your trading, then you should watch the first 5 minutes and not interact with it except in extremely favorable circumstances.

While many traders will wait for a completed 30 minutes before looking into ranges, it is statistically more likely that around 10 am, any false market movement will occur, leaving the 9:50 time frame in a strong relational position. After completing 9:30 to 9:50, you will want to take the time to determine the low and high values for the morning.

This will provide you with the clear indicators you need to determine boundaries that can indicate opportunities to take advantage of potential breakouts or primary trends. This will also allow you to set yourself up for any sharp reversal you expect to appear.

Depending on the results of the previous 20 minutes you will want to make a more confident move during this time period, either trading with or against the trend based on the indicators that you have seen. If you are planning to take advantage of this trading strategy, then this is the timeframe during which you will want to consider placing all of your trades for the day as if you wait even an extra 5 minutes then you will no longer be ahead of the pack and as a result your overall profits for the day will be seriously hampered because of it.

During this period, you are going to want to keep a close eye on your trades to ensure that the trends you were noticing early on continue on to maturity. While this might not seem like a long time to make a day's worth of profit, the truth of the matter is that if you got in by 9:50 am then you will have nearly a full hour to generate a profit using this timetable. What's more, if things are still proceeding smoothly then you can even hold out until 11 am, but only if the trends you predicted are proving exceedingly strong. During these instances, you will want to be ready to get rid of your holdings at a moment's notice if you want to prevent your profits from suddenly tilting in the opposite direction.

Despite the fact that if things are going well you won't have much to do during this period, it is important to never approach it in a manner that can be described as lackadaisical. You never know when the moment that things start moving the other direction is going to arrive which means you need to be ready and waiting for it when it does. It is important to have a clear exit point in mind going into this time frame and to never get greedy.

Strategy 21 -Order Flow Sequencing: Order Flow Sequencing was developed by a trader who worked at a number of the most well-known firms including Bear Stearns and Sungard Capital Markets. The goal with this strategy is to track and document what prices are driving the major players in a specific market to make which moves. This information will allow moderately successful traders to more clearly identify potential liquidity and risks with a greater level of transparency when it comes to the market as a whole.

When it comes to the major players in the market you prefer, it may help to think of them as the House when it comes to gambling. Sooner or later the house always wins and so too is it with the big money traders, if your trading against them, you will find it much more difficult to make money as opposed to traveling discreetly in their wake. Major players can include commercial traders, governments, financial institutions, merchant banks, regular banks and hedge funds, essentially anyone whose trades can lead to market imbalances due to solely to their actions.

Understanding the resulting trends can make it much easier to recognize and track major movements using techniques related to order flow. The result is an indication of the disruption that major players make when their trades go through due to their high volume, following these indications should be your goal as it will indicate that you are likely to be on the winning side of that particular trade.

Surprisingly few traders learn to understand and read the simple logic of how prices fluctuate in any given market but by using the order flow sequencing factor you can be one of them. Order flow sequencing first came in to popularity around the start of the twentieth century when a need for market generated information first started to gain importance in day to day trades. What makes it so effective in comparison to other indicator based methods is that other methods rely on information that is provided after the fact and order flow sequencing.

Strategy 22 -Pivot points: Charts are going to be so helpful to you when getting started in penny stock trading. And since there are plenty of charts available for any penny stocks that you wish to work with, you can easily get ahold of them for this next strategy. In most cases, you are going to work with the same few stocks each day that you trade. This allows you to become familiar with them, makes it easy to see their high and low points, and to make predictions about where the stock is going to head next.

Even for those who are just getting into penny stock trading, you can use some of the past charts to learn the information about trends of the company despite not having the charts of your own. You will be able to see the highs and lows and the overall trend of the stock and make your decisions based upon this.

Now, to make this strategy work, you will need to mark out the lows and the highs of this stock and then watch where the stock goes each day to find out where the highest or the lowest point is. Once you have determined these points, you should buy or sell the stock in the way that is appropriate for making a profit. When buying, you are going to make a profit when you are able to buy the stock at a low price.

So basically, you are going to look at these charts and try to figure out where the lowest and the highest points are. When the stock gets to the lowest point, it is time to enter the market and purchase the stock at a lower price, hopefully, lower than market value. You will then hold onto the stock for a bit, waiting for it to reach the high point on the chart, or at least higher than where you started so that you can make a profit when it's time to sell.

Strategy 23 -Penny Stock Scalping

While the extreme level of volatility that surrounds penny stocks means you need to be quick if you want to lock in profits with any degree of regularity, if you are on the ball then there is certainly money to be made by adopting a strategy that is based on scalping. What's more, as the overall volatility of the penny stock market is so high, the short-term market sentiment is considered the most trustworthy of the bunch which means this strategy has higher than average risk mitigation as well when compared with longer holding periods. It also allows you to more easily diversify by making it a relatively straightforward task to penetrate numerous different markets throughout a single day.

Another major part of scalping successfully is going to be setting your trading plan ahead of time and then following it to the letter when the time comes to execute on it. When prices line up and the time is ripe to truly make a profit, you need to be ready to act at the moment without having to finish figuring out all of the specific details at the last minute. Remember, the window for turning a profit on a specific cryptocurrency transaction can be extremely slim which means that you are going to want to choose your exit points very carefully in order to avoid losing out on the freshly minted profits.

Perhaps most importantly, scalping is all about making large numbers of low value trades all at once which is what makes penny stocks a natural choice. Furthermore, scalping strategies are typically going to be the most successful in the smaller timeframes, with the three-minute and the one-minute charts seeing the greatest amount of action on a regular basis and the five and 15-minute charts serving to confirm the early indicators. Technical analysis is going to be the order of the day as fundamental analysis will prove slow to be effective in this instance.

The biggest downside of scalping is the speed with which you are forced to react, along with the costs that come along with including the bid-offer spread which can serve to affect your profits as well if you aren't careful. This doesn't mean that the leverage still can't work against you, however, which is why it is important to cut your losses as quickly as possible if the trade appears to be turning against you. The best way to ensure you stay profitable with this style of trading is to make the most of each trend you discover by capitalizing on it as quickly as possible.

Bollinger bands: As a general rule, the closer the price in question is to the upper band, the more in danger the stock in question is of being overbought; while the closer it is to the lower band, the more oversold it is.

The squeeze is central to the success of a Bollinger band strategy in that when the bands come close together and constrict the moving average it is known as a squeeze. This, in turn, signals a period of low volatility and is considered by traders to be a sign that increased volatility is incoming, along with all of the possibilities that it brings. On the other hand, the wider apart the bands are, the more likely the change is that they decrease in volatility overall, which means it is likely a good time to exit a trade.

The goal, then, is to pinpoint period where the prices touch a point that is between the pair of standard deviations. Once this occurs you will want to use a moving average that is set to 200 as the guideline that will allow you to monitor the trend as it changes over time. If the price rises above this point, then you will be able to profit from any long positions that you may take, while if it drops below this point short positions will be profitable to various degrees. If a candle forms inside the deviations then the trend is likely to continue while if it forms outside then the reverse is likely to occur instead.

When these conditions are met, you can rest assured that entering a trade when the next candle forms is a safe choice as it will only open you up to a small amount of additional risk. You will, however, still want to place a stop loss based on the apparent strength of the trend you are keeping an eye on. You will also want to set a target at the point that marks the average of the Bollinger bands, with a second target at the line of the Bollinger band the trend is more likely to intersect with. This strategy is known to be extremely effective, as long as you take into account the price only as it relates to the moving average of 200. As it can be complicated to get a handle on, at first, it is suggested that you practice with this strategy using a number of smaller trades until you are comfortable with the process.

Longer strategy: While not quite as short as the traditional scalping strategy, the one-hour strategy works off a strict 50 pips goal for each trade so its overall effectiveness balances out. As the timeframe is naturally longer, it is recommended that you only use it with stocks that are experiencing a lull in volatility. Whether buying or selling, if the current trend is bullish and the price is touching the band, you will want to generate an order using a stop loss that is 35 pips lower (or higher depending on the trend).

From there, you will then want to set an exit point that is 50 pips further along in the direction of the trend to guarantee that you cash out when you hit your profit goal. This doesn't mean you can set it and forget it, however, as you will also want to be on hand to sell if the trend reverses or if the price reaches the other band.

Extreme scalping: This system requires Bollinger bands that are set to twenty-one periods with a standard deviation of two. It is useful for timetables of one minute that have an RSI of fourteen, seventy, thirty. The goal here is to wait for the price to rise above one of the Bollinger bands while at the same time have the RSI increase to above seventy or to below thirty. The ideal target, in this case, is the dead center of the pair of bands with a pair of stop-loss five to seven pips higher and lower. As with the other strategies, practicing is recommended as it is more complicated than it may first appear.

CONCLUSION

Armed with the investing knowledge in this book, you can turn small amounts of money into fantastically large amounts with very little effort. The biggest takeaway from this book is to focus on the long-term market as a whole. Funds managed by experts usually always fail to beat the consistent returns of a low fee index fund over the long term, so all one would need to do to make millions is let compound interest work for them.

Making a plan will be useless, however, if you don't work to cultivate the proper mindset for trading prior to getting started, thereby maximizing your effectiveness as much as possible. As such, you are going to want to keep the following tips in mind to ensure your results are as positive as possible. Here are some of the tips that you can employ for success.

Stay flexible: The stock market is a volatile place which means that if you ever hope to be successful when investing in it then you are going to need to remain ready to pivot at a moment's notice. The market can change in a matter of minutes which means a stock on a long-running profitability streak can suddenly turn around and become worthless, literally overnight. This means that if you want to succeed you are going to need to limit the influence the past has on your decisions and instead focus on the information available in the present and what it will likely mean for the future. Essentially, you are going to need to be ready to ditch investments that are turning on you and also reevaluate previous choices if you hope to see reliable results in the long term.

Commit to a plan: The plan that you end up creating is going to be critical to your success in the long term, but only if you stick with it every time you choose an investment. While it won't always lead you to success with every trade, if you create it using the proper criteria then it should lead you to make profitable trades greater than 50 percent of the time which means you will win out in the end as long as you stick with it religiously. Furthermore, knowing the acceptable criteria when it comes to selling and buying at a given moment is crucial to ensure that you will be able to take advantage of emerging trends at a time when it will be able to do you the most good.

Have measured expectations: While it is possible to grow rich from investing in the stock market, it is unlikely that this will be a process that happens overnight. Rather, most people who find success there slowly amass assets overtime by holding on to profitable trades and getting rid of those that don't pan out before they can generate too much loss.

Additionally, it is likely to take you a prolonged period of time before you get the hang of things which means you should expect to post a losing record for the first few months you start investing in stocks while you are learning the ropes. It is also important to keep in mind that this is normal and stick with it if you hope to eventually cross from the red into the black. Going into the process with a realistic idea of what it's going to take in order to be successful is an ideal way of ensuring that the learning curve will be as manageable as possible.

Choose personalized strategies: Just because you hear about a strategy that is guaranteed to work because someone else found success with it is no real indicator that it is going to work for you. While there is certainly no reason not to give it a try, it is important to ensure that it stands up to your personal standards and matches your natural investment inclinations as well. If it doesn't it will be unlikely to generate the results you are looking for, no matter how much of a sure thing it is purported to be.

Instead, it is always important to be on the lookout for new strategies that line up with your personal inclinations to use as a stepping stone to stock investing success as opposed to barriers that need to be circumvented in order to see any results. Remaining true to yourself is always going to be most reliable way to see positive results in the long run.

Be disciplined: It is common for many new traders to go after one type of stock or specifics stocks simply because they have a gut feeling about them. The sad truth of the matter is that gut feelings rarely, if ever, pay out effectively. As such, if you follow this scattershot approach you are going to end up making it more difficult to turn a profit in both the short and the long-term. What's worse, if you do end up finding success with this process then all you will be learning is bad habits which will translate to fewer overall successes in the future. Instead of focusing on your gut, it is important to focus on building the discipline you need to make the right choices in the moment even if you gut is telling you something else. While this will likely be hard at first, it will get easier with time.

Seek absolute truth: It doesn't matter if youu feel that the price of a given stock is too low or too high, the only thing you can reliably focus on is the price as it currently stands in the moment. If the facts say that a stock should be valued higher than it currently is then you will want to buy and if it is lower than you will want to sell, end of story. You need to remain impartial about these facts and simply do what they tell you. Developing an attachment to a given stock is only going to hurt your results in the long run.

Focus on logic: After you have formed a successful plan, following it precisely with each trade that you make will always be the most logical choice. This means that even if the trade doesn't end up working out the way you expected, you should still be pleased with yourself as long as you did what made the most sense in the moment. Going off book is only going to lead to failure, far more often than it leads to success. Instead of raging against failed trades, simply look at them as the statistical balance to the other more profitable trades you are likely to make more than 50 percent of the time assuming your plan is sound.

Sometimes doing nothing is the right choice: If you have reason to believe a specific stock is overvalued then you will want to sell, if it is undervalued then you will want to buy. The same principles goes for when a stock is stuck in the middle of the road, in these circumstances then the best course of action is going to be to wait for a stronger signal to appear to indicate a movement in one direction or another. Many new traders find that waiting about without making a move is one of the hardest things to do.

Making trades just to trade is always going to be folly, however, because if the market isn't moving much at all, or if it is moving so much that determining a clear course of action, then waiting for things to normalize is always going to lead to more reliable profits in the long-term. Your goal should always be to make trades for the sake of profit, not just to trade for trading's sake.

Understand that there are no sure things: The odds of finding a system that will accurately predict trades 100 percent of the time, or even 90 percent of the time are extremely small. In fact, you have a better chance of winning the lottery or being struck by lightning than of getting anywhere close to those numbers. There are just too many variables to consider at all times, even before you factor in chance and pure, dumb, luck. Rather than wasting time looking for the impossible, you will find much better results by looking for a plan that you can rely on and just take the additional loss that you will see with a grain of salt.

The next step is to begin to apply what you have learned during the course of this book and get started right away. Our suggestion is always to open up a demo account on a broker and make a few tries before putting real money into it. Remember that you should never risk more than what you can afford to lose, so manage your capital wisely.

We hope that you find these lessons valuable and acquired the information you were looking for. Letting your money work for you will give you an incredible feeling, especially at the beginning when you make the first gains. We are thrilled for you to start, and we cannot wait to see your results coming in!